info@kinfolk.com
www.kinfolk.com

Kinfolk Magazine
328 NE Failing Street
Portland, Oregon 97212 USA
Telephone: 503-946-8400

Printed in Canada

———

Publication Design by Charlotte Heal
Cover Photograph by Neil Bedford

KINFOLK

TOAST

WOMEN

MEN

HOUSE&HOME

WWW.TOA.ST

NATHAN WILLIAMS

Editor in Chief & Brand Director

GEORGIA FRANCES KING	**CHARLOTTE HEAL**
Editor	*Creative Director*
GAIL O'HARA	**ANJA VERDUGO**
Managing Editor	*Art Director*
DOUG BISCHOFF	**KATIE SEARLE-WILLIAMS**
Business Operations	*Business Manager*
NATHAN TICKNOR	**JENNIFER JAMES WRIGHT**
Operations Manager	*Ouur Design Director*
JULIE POINTER	**JESSICA GRAY**
Community Director	*Community Manager*
PAIGE BISCHOFF	**ERIC DAVIS**
Accounts Payable & Receivable	*Web Administrator*
AMANDA JANE JONES	**JOANNA HAN**
Founding Designer	*Contributing Editor*
KELSEY SNELL	**ANDREA SLONECKER**
Proofreader	*Recipe Editor*
ANNA PERLING	**BRIANNA KOVAN**
Editorial Assistant	*Editorial Assistant*
HANNA FOX	**KATARINA BERGER**
Editorial Assistant	*Operations Assistant*
GRETA LICKTEIG	**NATHANIEL SAVAGE**
Operations Assistant	*Art Assistant*

————

SUBSCRIBE

KINFOLK IS PUBLISHED FOUR TIMES A YEAR
TO SUBSCRIBE, VISIT WWW.KINFOLK.COM/SUBSCRIBE OR EMAIL US AT SUBSCRIBE@KINFOLK.COM

CONTACT US

IF YOU HAVE QUESTIONS OR COMMENTS, PLEASE WRITE TO US AT INFO@KINFOLK.COM
FOR ADVERTISING INQUIRIES, GET IN TOUCH AT ADVERTISING@KINFOLK.COM

www.kinfolk.com

GIVE THE GIFT OF SMALL GATHERINGS

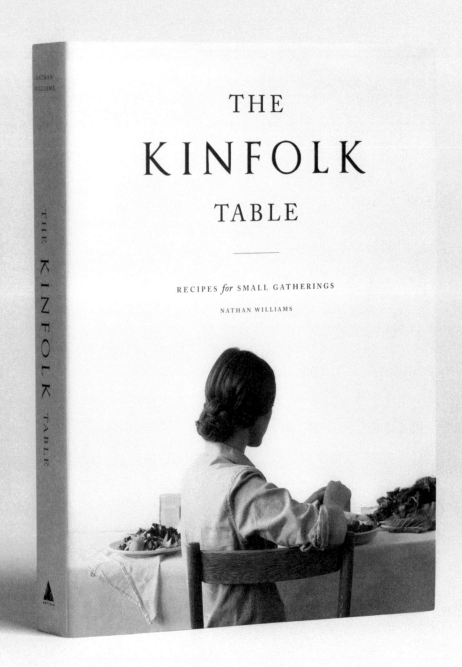

WHEREVER BOOKS ARE SOLD

Ouur

ISSUE FOURTEEN CONTRIBUTORS

ANDERSEN M STUDIO
Photographer & Designer
London, United Kingdom

TRAVIS ELBOROUGH
Writer
London, United Kingdom

VERONICA MARTIN
Writer
Portland, Oregon

UTA BARTH
Photographer
Los Angeles, California

MARGARET EVERTON
Writer
Portland, Oregon

MAMI OONISHI
Stylist
Osaka, Japan

KYLE BEAN
Set Designer
London, United Kingdom

PARKER FITZGERALD
Photographer
Portland, Oregon

GIULIA PINES
Writer
Berlin, Germany

NEIL BEDFORD
Photographer
London, United Kingdom

ROSE FORDE
Stylist
London, United Kingdom

MARK SANDERS
Photographer
London, United Kingdom

LAURA BRAUN
Photographer
London, United Kingdom

ALICE GAO
Photographer
New York, New York

ANDERS SCHØNNEMANN
Photographer
Copenhagen, Denmark

LUISA BRIMBLE
Photographer
Sydney, Australia

JAMES GEER
Photographer
Melbourne, Australia

DANIEL SEARING
Writer
Washington, D.C.

LOUISA THOMSEN BRITS
Writer
East Sussex, United Kingdom

IAIN GRAHAM
Food Stylist
London, United Kingdom

JOHN STANLEY
Writer
London, United Kingdom

JAMES CARTWRIGHT
Writer
London, United Kingdom

LAURIE GRIFFITHS
Photographer
Brighton, United Kingdom

ANNU SUBRAMANIAN
Writer
New York, New York

HELEN CATHCART
Photographer
London, United Kingdom

HIDEAKI HAMADA
Photographer
Osaka, Japan

AARON TILLEY
Photographer
London, United Kingdom

RACHEL CAULFIELD
Stylist
London, United Kingdom

MERIJN HOS
Artist
Utrecht, The Netherlands

TRINETTE & CHRIS
Photographers
San Francisco, California

WAI CHU
Writer
New York, New York

KIRSTIN JACKSON
Writer
Oakland, California

HELLE WALSTED
Stylist & Producer
Copenhagen, Denmark

LIZ CLAYTON
Writer
Brooklyn, New York

SARAH JACOBY
Illustrator
Philadelphia, Pennsylvania

RAHEL WEISS
Photographer
London, United Kingdom

KATRIN COETZER
Illustrator
Cape Town, South Africa

KATE S. JORDAN
Prop Stylist
Pound Ridge, New York

WICHMANN + BENDTSEN
Photographers
Copenhagen, Denmark

DAVID COGGINS
Writer
New York, New York

MIKKEL KARSTAD
Writer
Copenhagen, Denmark

AMY WOODROFFE
Writer
Melbourne, Australia

DEANE W. CURTIN
Writer
St. Paul, Minnesota

STEPHANIE ROSENBAUM KLASSEN
Writer
Sonoma, California

TAO WU
Photographer
Hefei, China

ROKAS DARULIS
Photographer
London, United Kingdom

PETER KRAGBALLE
Photographer
Copenhagen, Denmark

DIANA YEN
Writer & Stylist
New York, New York

MYKITA

HANDMADE IN BERLIN

MYKITA SHOP BERLIN Rosa-Luxemburg-Str. 6 / Budapester Str. 38-50 MYKITA SHOP CARTAGENA
Carrera 5 #35-70 MYKITA SHOP MONTERREY Jose Vasconcelos 150 PB-6D MYKITA SHOP NEW YORK 109 Crosby Street
MYKITA SHOP PARIS 2 Rue du Pas de la Mule MYKITA SHOP TOKYO 5-11-6 Jingumae MYKITA SHOP VIENNA Neuer Markt 14
MYKITA SHOP ZERMATT Bahnhofstrasse 5 MYKITA SHOP ZURICH Langstrasse 187

WELCOME

Winter is a season for reinvention. The quietness that falls like a fresh blanket of snow is the perfect opportunity to reconsider our relationship with both the landscape and ourselves. It's a time to look back on the past, make some changes and reemerge from our self-imposed cocoons rested and invigorated. For the Winter Issue, we've revitalized ourselves and looked at the season through fresh eyes.

Family is paramount this time of year, but reaching out beyond your clan can foster an even stronger sense of community. We look at how numerous countries from Peru to Iran celebrate the solstice, study Naples' custom of pay-it-forward coffees and introduce our first regular neighborhood feature—the district of Peckham in South East London—to learn how we can nurture our local lives.

During the chilly season, the purpose of our home fluctuates between revelry and refuge, from sleep to celebration. As the days grow shorter and we retreat inside to nest, creating a comfortable environment becomes central to our happiness. A cohort of lighting designers teaches us how to best illuminate our spaces, we look at homes in Denmark and Australia—two locations with very different approaches to winter—to see how they work with the elements, and we think about how our kitchens change meaning when the sky darkens.

Despite the urge to hibernate, there are plenty of ways to keep your engine running both indoors and out, such as trying your arm at fencing, joining a professional snowball-fighting league or telling stories through shadow puppetry.

This is also the season when our pantries swell with staples and our fridge is stocked with all kinds of holiday treats. In this issue, we reconsider fruitcake's unfortunate reputation, play board games with sweets and guide you through an all-day cookie-baking affair (with only one oven). Overeating and imbibing are par for the course with so many festivities, so we also provide a mental palate cleanser via our inaugural academic excerpt, Professor Deane Curtin's "Authentic Presence to Food."

A portion of this issue is dedicated to exploring the meaning of light (or the lack of it in wintertime) and its influence on our health and creativity. Artists, designers and scientists weigh in on the sun's importance, such as Danish-Icelandic luminary Olafur Eliasson and a neuroscientist/artist duo that's studying the effects of sunlight on our mental and physical well-being.

Whether you're toasty in front of a fireplace or zipping down a mountain, we hope this issue provides you with some innovative ways to make the most of these frosty days and reinvent both yourself and the season.

NATHAN WILLIAMS AND GEORGIA FRANCES KING

Community

Home

MASTHEAD
6

CONTRIBUTORS
10

WELCOME
13

CREDITS
158

This time of year contains a stockpot full of traditions and a chance to make new ones. From childhood to neighborhood, there are plenty of opportunities to learn from other cultures and their cozy customs.

With only a little light peering through the windows to coax us out from under our duvets, now is the time to refocus our attention on what lies between our walls and the people who dwell within them.

ESSAY:
SHAPE SHIFTERS
24

CULTURE:
ITALY'S CAFFÈ SOSPESO
27

HISTORY:
SOLSTICE TRADITIONS
122

NEIGHBORHOOD:
PECKHAM, LONDON
148

EVENTS:
KINFOLK GATHERINGS
156

ESSAY:
BEFORE THE DAY STARTS
18

ESSAY:
WINTER'S KITCHEN
20

HISTORY:
HOT WATER BOTTLES
21

PROFILE:
EDITOR JULIE BOUCHERAT
28

INTERVIEW:
CHEF MIKKEL KARSTAD
48

ESSAY:
HOW TO HIBERNATE
74

FEATURE:
THE MEANING OF LIGHT
100

HOME TOURS:
DENMARK AND AUSTRALIA
134

Work

Frosty evenings and dreary days are a good chance to be productive by working on projects you may have neglected. Keeping your creative flame alight will sustain your motivation's spark.

ESSAY:
COLORING THE GRAY
26

INTERVIEW:
ARTIST OLAFUR ELIASSON
110

INTERVIEW:
LIGHTING DESIGNERS
112

PHOTO ESSAY:
COVERING OUR COMMUTE
124

Play

Wintertime recreation falls into two categories: those that require speed, agility and a good set of gloves, and those that are best enjoyed in front of a fireplace with a warm beverage topped with rum.

CULTURE:
JAPAN'S YUKIGASSEN
34

PHOTO ESSAY:
CANDY BOARD GAMES
40

PHOTO ESSAY:
INDOOR FENCING
58

PHOTO ESSAY:
THE SOLACE OF SOAKING
68

PHOTO ESSAY:
PEAK AMBITION
94

PHOTO ESSAY:
AURORA FOLKLORE
116

Food

Keeping the pantry stocked full of comforting staples is a tasty way to conquer the cold. It's a time for the oven to be roaring from morning till night, wafting out a stream of starchy delights.

OPINION:
UNEXPECTED PAIRINGS
30

RECIPE: TURKEY SANDWICH
WITH CRANBERRY CHUTNEY
32

RECIPE: SOLE AND BRUSSELS
SPROUTS WITH TARRAGON
56

EXCERPT:
AUTHENTIC PRESENCE TO FOOD
80

INTERVIEW:
PROFESSOR DEANE CURTIN
83

RECIPE: CHESTNUT
COOKIE SANDWICHES
88

RECIPE: PISTACHIO ROSEWATER
SNOWBALL COOKIES
90

RECIPE: MAPLE PECAN
SHORTBREAD COOKIES
92

Starters

WORDS
MARGARET EVERTON

Before the Day Starts

Making the most of morning's predawn hours can be the best way to start the day, whether it's for reading, ruminating or romanticizing.

The early winter mornings are dark and quiet. Although your warm bed beckons you to climb back inside, starting your day *before* the day can leave you enlightened and ready to meet life's later requirements that rise with the sun. It's not a time to get ahead at work or skim your social media feed—those can wait, as can the laundry, the shopping list and the call to your mother. These things will get done, but the predawn hours offer you the chance to do something for yourself and should therefore be protected.

Countless other early birds have refused to let menial daily tasks bully this golden time. Before entering her studio for the day, Georgia O'Keeffe woke at dawn to her dogs barking, warmed up with tea and then took a walk. Henry David Thoreau ventured out into the frigid morning to hear the first birdsongs. While his wife slept in, P.G. Wodehouse did calisthenics on his front porch before reading pop fiction over coffee cake, toast and tea.

Others rose early to pursue their passions before beginning their normal life. Sylvia Plath woke at 5 a.m. to write before tending to her two young children, as did Toni Morrison, who raised her two sons while working in a publishing house. ("It's not being *in* the light," she said. "It's being there *before it arrives*.") His days filled with business, Frank Lloyd Wright developed his architectural designs from 4 to 7 a.m., and Immanuel Kant meditated over a pipe and weak tea before heading to the local university to teach science.

Rising at the same time every day with ceremony can establish a ritual (plus, the consistency helps prevent you from giving up). Whether you wake to work on a passion project or indulge in doing nothing, beginning with a routine makes this time distinct. The night before, prep your French press or set out your loose-leaf tea so all you have to do in the morning is stumble in and blearily boil water. Listen to Glenn Gould's version of Bach's *Goldberg Variations*—or Daft Punk if you prefer. If you crave a more ascetic start, put on a sweater and slip over to your desk without a sound. The morning may be cold, but you'll warm as you awaken and devote a fresh and unadulterated mind to your fascinations.

And if you can't rouse yourself despite your best intentions? Perhaps you incessantly push the snooze button or decide that no amount of predawn enlightenment is worth the lull you fall into by midafternoon. Thankfully, the fullness of life is not proportionate to how early you rise. Proust slept during the day and worked through the night, George Gershwin came home after evening parties to compose music until dawn, and George Sand often left her lovers' beds to write in the midnight silence that inspired her.

Whether their gravitational pull was toward morning or night, these visionaries all established a daily space only for themselves and refused to let their creative spirits hibernate. Their efforts were both large and small, but always deliberate. If all you do is wake up 15 minutes earlier to sip and not gulp your coffee, then you're opening yourself up to a more intimate life. As the poet Johann Wolfgang von Goethe once said, "The early morning hours have gold in their mouth." And who doesn't want to be dusted with gold?

WORDS
KATIE SEARLE-WILLIAMS

Winter's Kitchen

—

When the crisper months drift in, we are drawn to the home's culinary heart. The oven provides us with a special kind of warmth and a constant flow of sweet and savory comfort.

Our homes are living organisms, our lifeblood: They breathe, consume and sleep in synchronization with time's passing. The seasons turn like a clock, and as each rolls around a new variety of liveliness fills the air: Bare feet scamper in and out of a slamming screen door in the summer while boots shuffle and shake off snow in the entryway in the winter. Year in and year out, these fluctuations happen to rooms as well as their inhabitants, and the most noticeable changes occur in the kitchen.

We do all we can to avoid the oven in the warmer months, grazing on lighter fare by making chilled soups and salads. If baking must be done, the goods are left on the sill to cool. Much of our diet is also sourced externally, away from the kitchen entirely: We snack as we tend the garden, harvest roadside berries on walks or gather freshly picked goods as we wander through outdoor markets. The windows are flung open and we relocate to the cooler areas of the house or outside into the balmy air to munch and crunch.

When temperatures drop, the opposite happens—the whole family swarms to the kitchen, the reappointed centralized hearth of the home. The oven is always on call, spilling forth scents of molasses and treats galore. Our food becomes sourced internally from what's on hand in the pantry or comes from the chard bed located right outside the door.

During these colder days, visitors tend to congregate at the counter, waiting for the next batch of comfort food to appear on a plate in front of them (or just to bask in the stove's enveloping heat). The kitchen becomes a resting place, a gathering place, where conversations are deep and long and come complete with a warm cocoa or mulled wine in hand. Because life is less hurried, the discussions are not focused on to-dos and surface matters, but more on considerations that have been ruminating for some time.

The bones of the room change as well. The chairs and stools that had been dragged out to the porch make their way back to the kitchen island, the curtains are drawn and the lights dimmed. The room feels fuller too, with shadows plumping out the once-airy space. Speckled candlelight splashes ruddy cheeks, and any stiffness in the air that may have blown in with a draft wafts away in this glow of warmth.

If you were to check the pulse of a house, you might examine sounds, scents, scratches and smudges. Although the tempo of the scuffs and stains differs from room to room, in the winter you'll find the most resonant beats emanating from the kitchen. And even in the midst of constant transformation, the essence of this space as a source of nourishment will always remain steady.

ILLUSTRATION: KATRIN COETZER

WORDS
LOUISA THOMSEN BRITS

Gezelligheid

This untranslatable Dutch word expresses the homey feeling of defrosting toes and tempers.

TYPE: Abstract noun
LANGUAGE: Dutch
PRONUNCIATION: "huh-zell-ich-hait"
ETYMOLOGY: Derived from *gezel*: a companion or friend; someone who belongs.
MEANING: *Gezelligheid* is at the core of Dutch culture. It's an atmosphere, a vibe, a serendipitous togetherness, an aesthetic, a relaxed mood, a feeling of flow, a sense of belonging. No matter where you are or what you're doing, it describes the sensation of being at home. You'll find it where the coffee is hot, the beer is cold and a fire is roaring.
USE: Gezelligheid captures the feeling of being in a bookshop on a rainy afternoon, the low-key jubilance of Friday evening drinks on the couch or a lantern-lit front porch. To describe a person, place or gathering that has gezelligheid, use the adjective *gezellig*: It's gezellig to hang out with an old friend you haven't seen for a while, and fresh flowers or lit candles on a windowsill are also gezellig.

WORDS
GIULIA PINES

A Hot Water Bottle History

An eco-friendly alternative to the electric blanket, the hot water bottle has had a treacherous path to popularity.

As you suffer through cold winter days by hugging your scarf close, lost in an over-size robe or sweater, your one consolation is the cocoon of warmth that awaits you that evening in bed. There, embraced by quilts and goose down, it feels as if the day's chill can no longer penetrate. Stretching your feet to the end of the mattress, your toes hit something soft and sloshy: a hot water bottle, tucked between the sheets. Now a ubiquitous household object across countless cultures, the hot water bottle took centuries to arrive in the cozy form we know it as today.

Once upon a time, stuffing your bed with hot coals directly from the fireplace was the only way to warm your sheets. Unless you had a masochist for a house-maid, she would have done this by taking two round copper or brass pans welded together at the edges and mounted on a handle, and filling them with embers. Instead of smoldering at our feet for hours, they were mostly swiped quickly between the sheets in the evening, as a night spent with one of these contraptions could lead to serious consequences: When filled with coals, embers or ashes, they could reach scalding temperatures, inflict serious burns and even cause fires.

The switch to stoneware bottles in the 19th century allowed for toasty toes without medical treatment from the Middle Ages (or what might have passed for it back then). These sturdy vessels could be filled with boiling water instead of burning embers, making them slightly safer and more portable. This way they could be taken to bed the entire night, often wrapped in fabric or fitted with a specially knitted cover. Still, a ceramic bottle was hard and cumbersome: not exactly a welcome bedfellow.

Fast forward to the beginning of the Industrial Age and the subsequent invention of vulcanized rubber, which would later be used for car tires, the soles of shoes and—you guessed it—hot water bottles. When organic chemist and inventor Slavoljub Eduard Penkala patented his 1903 design for what he called the *termofor* (the Polish word for "hot water bottle"), the ultimate low-tech heating device arrived in its current, less dangerous form.

The modern hot water bottle has come a long way from its days as an instrument of torture in disguise. Hot coals have been replaced by water, metal with rubber and pain with pleasure. Although these floppy rubber bottles may look like something you'd find in your grandmother's guest room, they're enjoying a revival among those looking for a low-energy solution to staying snug in bed all night long. It proves once again that sometimes the simplest solutions are still the best.

PHOTOGRAPH: PARKER FITZGERALD

WORDS
GEORGIA FRANCES KING

Tinsel Tussle

Losing yourself in a mundane task is a fine way to unwind during the harried holiday season.

When it's time to decorate the almighty piney pillar of yuletide, I take a Zen-like pleasure in being the one to untangle the tinsel. While others compete for the dainty glass baubles, you can find me cross-legged in the corner combing my fingers through the metallic dreadlocks of Christmas. Regardless of what kind of debauchery might be unfolding—short-circuiting strands of lights, cousins jostling for the esteemed right to crown the tree with an apathetic-looking angel—I'm always left to myself and my hugely satisfying unraveling. During this time, I'm granted a few moments of respite from everything chaotic that the season brings. I let myself hone in on the subtle knots and intricate waves of the synthetic mass, weaving the strands in and around and under and over and out, lulling myself into a calmness not even a fourth mug of eggnog can encourage. What starts as a bird's nest of highly flammable twine unfurls into a length of glitzy string proportionate to my sense of gratification. It's taught me that it's okay to take a short break from the frivolity of the season and let the afternoon be humdrum—it can unwind more than just the tinsel.

WORDS
KIRSTIN JACKSON

Allergic to Christmas

Some piney afflictions can be overcome using the powers of a hot glue gun, some tumbleweeds and a bit of motherly ingenuity.

Miles away from the gingerbread and roaring fireplaces I would one day hold dear, I spent my first three Christmases sick in the hospital. No one knew why. It could not have been because of the actual holiday—we were Scandinavian-German-American Lutherans after all. The season's spices of cardamom and nutmeg flowed though our blood. We were born knowing the words to all the carols. My mother owned more Santa figurines than shoes. We chopped down our own tree in the Sierras every winter.

But the year I turned four, we didn't make it to the Sierras. We didn't get a tree, and I didn't get sick. So when my Aunt Lin casually mentioned to my mom over a hot toddy that Uncle Dave was allergic to certain types of trees, my mother put two and two together: I was allergic to the pine beacon of Christmas.

My family refused to let the news best them and their festive decorating plans. The next year we still went to the cabin and chopped down a tree, but we left it outside my bedroom window and adorned its limbs with pinecones spread with peanut butter. Despite the birds that the window display attracted, my young heart yearned for something I could gaze at in the living room. A few years later, my parents bought an official Charlie Brown Christmas tree. It had around 25 spindly limbs that could only support a single strand of lights—you could see the presents beneath it, the wall behind it and the entire tree all at the same time.

Then my mother got creative. On our next trip to the cabin, she chopped down a manzanita instead of a pine. Using one bush as a base and the others for volume, she hot-glue-gunned the branches in a triangle and spray-painted the DIY Christmas bush white. Another time we rounded up some tumbleweeds (or rather, I scrunched down in the backseat while my parents pulled over to hunt the diaspora): Mom wired three of them together and spray-painted them gold. We carefully hung its delicate limbs with tinsel and lights and patiently explained to our relatives that yes, we did indeed forage tumbleweeds on Southern California back roads.

While I tried not to let my sighs of evergreen envy and arboreal longing hinder my friends' festive spirit, my parents broke holiday traditions to make our own. Now whenever I spot a decorated tree that makes me pine for pine, I remind myself that few mothers have done for their child's Christmas—with a pruner, glue gun, wire, handsaw and a can of spray-paint—what my mother did for mine.

WORDS
ANNU SUBRAMANIAN

Shape Shifters

When the temperature drops, our bodies change: the way we hold them, the way we dress them and the way we move in them.

Our date books lack ink in winter, as if the weather is as aware of us as we are of it. It offers us a reprieve from summer's outdoor happy hours and the autumn weekends away: a season-sanctioned rest period. Winter turns us in—indoors, inward, intimate—and in these ways causes us to shift form. Like the leaves and long evenings, certain qualities of ours seem to fade and make way for a new identity.

It might be easy to see a sameness in ourselves throughout the year, and it's a tired dig to point out the slight weight gain that seems inevitable as the temperature dives. But something more beautiful is at play, because in winter we are in flux. We assume a spectrum of textures, silhouettes, structures, sizes and sounds that belong exclusively to the season.

The most quickly identifiable change is in our stature. Where summer encourages a tall gait, we huddle closer in winter. Summer is for holding hands; winter for holding tight. Arms draw in a partner's waist, heads find comfort nestling on a shoulder and couples hunch in unison against the elements. A busy street is a flood of dark tones with petite people appearing enlarged as they navigate under heavy layers. Even a short walk against harsh wind makes us tear up, leaving weather-weary eyes looking dewy and bright. When eyelashes first catch snowflakes, they make our eyes flash glints of light like an ornament. And as those flakes melt

into droplets, pooling at the base of our eyelashes, we appear refreshed. Smiles have seasons too—in winter they're constricted, too cold to expand.

How can people say we lose color in the winter when noses turn red? When scarlet rushes to our cheeks? When blonde hair naturally darkens and black hair becomes an even starker sable? Palms turn pink, fingertips almost yellow, blue veins bright against flesh. We rarely associate winter with color, yet they are inextricably linked.

Our gestures change too, even when we're indoors: Notice how you dress, how you eat, where your hands rest. Suddenly people always seem to be wrapping themselves: in shawls, in thick blankets, in second layers, tugging the bulky part of a sweater or going around once more with a scarf. In hot weather sleep is restless and a shared bed can be a battle of limbs, but in winter bodies wrap around each other with ease, breath rising and falling in tandem. Is there a sound more emblematic than the *stomp stomp stomp* of boots shaking off sleet upon arriving home? Or the sigh of a zipper being released and the rustling of a heavy jacket being removed? Of a fireplace crackling like Pop Rocks or the uneven whir of an old-fashioned radiator?

For all its squalls and storms, this weather is the only stretch when we wear these qualities, as though we unpacked them with our heaviest sweaters. And remarkably, they're a lovely fit.

ARTWORK: MERIJN HOS, PHOTOGRAPHS: ANJA VERDUGO

A STEAMING CUP WARMS FROM THE INSIDE OUT

BREATH FORMS CLOUDS OF FROST LIKE SPEECH BUBBLES

SUMMER IS FOR HOLDING HANDS, WINTER FOR HOLDING TIGHT

PERMANENT RESIDENCE IS FOUND UNDER THE COVERS

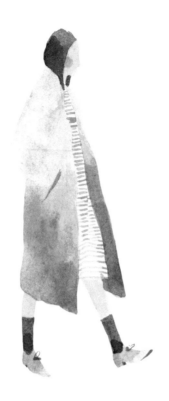

WORDS
VERONICA MARTIN

Coloring
the Gray

---

*The foundations for a winter wardrobe
begin with cool neutrals, but adding bursts
of color can enliven even the coldest of days.*

We often try to distinguish a particular season's beauty by dressing accordingly. In the winter we express ourselves through colors and textures evocative of the type of darkness that sets in early and stays late: gnarled wool, sumptuous fuzzy cashmere, heavy gabardine, fleece-lined boots. We try to channel the season's elegance with our changing daily uniform of the perfect coat and boot combination, the right glove-to-scarf-to-hat ratio or with silken layers beneath thick capes that act as wearable blankets we throw around our shoulders.

But dressing with winter's subdued palette creates a layered landscape begging for a slash of sunlit tone. During the darker months, the mind finds refuge in patches of perceived sunlight on the body: linden green, ice-tipped pink, Yves Klein blue. Each color acts as an entry point into understanding, a kind of seasonal synesthesia.

Winter is a season to add pigment in small doses. Few designers create a collection without some buoyant, almost artificial hue to strike through the monochrome: mango tango orange, flamingo pink or a broad swath of spring sky blue. The pervasive gray of winter can paralyze us while color offers the potential of movement.

Slip your fingers into a pair of burnt orange gloves and see how it changes your intimacy with the landscape. Stand in winter's quiet panorama and observe its icy gray blues, forest greens and oxblood reds. The silence that accompanies such seasonally bleak geography finds its antidote in color. The orange accenting your hands amplifies the rest of the world's hues, and by unraveling the million tiny threads inherent in just one color, you begin to see the world with different eyes.

Take off a pair of orange-tinted ski goggles and you'll find the world has turned the opposite tincture, blue. Unlike the heat of orange, blue holds within it an element of darkness, the presence and absence of light at play. A blue room seems bigger and navy suggests greater authority. It's the color of cold but also suggests shade. Colors, both artificially seen in the fabric of our clothes and located in the natural world, amplify what they surround: Cold colors are seen to retreat from us, while warmer ones approach.

Although the winter wardrobe should have its foundations in utility, we don't need to arrive at each season's threshold with only the suggested arsenal of black wool coats, gray turtleneck sweaters and sturdy chestnut boots. Folding light into our winter wardrobe turns an elemental fear of darkness into something of an embrace. As Oscar Wilde said, "Mere color, unspoiled by meaning, and unallied with definite form, can speak to the soul in a thousand different ways."

WORDS
ANNA PERLING

A Cup of Goodwill

The Neapolitan custom of caffè sospeso brings a community-minded meaning to "two cups a day."

Naples, the capital of Italy's southern region of Campania, isn't too different from the rest of the nation when it comes to its reverence for coffee. Wherever you are in the country, you'll witness the daily pilgrimage to espresso bars if you're up early enough. Countless commuters—whether they're in suits, hard hats or high heels—stream in and out of the infinite cafés, seamlessly reentering the street's flow of foot traffic with brighter eyes and pastries in hand.

But something unusual sometimes happens to coffee orders in Naples. Instead of the standard request for *un* caffè, it often becomes *due*—customers order two coffees instead of one. They drink the first and request the other as a *caffè sospeso*, a "suspended coffee" that remains in limbo as a pending order, waiting to be claimed by other coffee drinkers who may not be able to afford a cup of their own. Anyone may inquire if there is a

caffè sospeso at the bar and receive a suspended drink. The custom provides an anonymous way to help others and has garnered attention around the world: It's now possible to pay for suspended coffee in cafés from Melbourne to Oslo.

Italy's coffee rituals go back to the 1700s when one of Europe's first coffee shops was built in Venice. Two hundred more quickly popped up along the canals and the café tradition took hold. Unsurprisingly, Italy also first patented the espresso machine in the early 1900s, steeping espresso drinks even more thoroughly into the daily lives of Italians.

At a certain point the rituals, habits and routines that punctuate our lives become so second nature that they start to go unnoticed. Accordingly, Italians have developed a slew of coffee-drinking methods so ingrained into their caffeinated culture that no one dares question them. Requests for ristretto, macchiato,

caffè or cappuccino are placed at the bar, not with a "please" beforehand but simply the designated amount. Exact change is expected, as is standing—a seat often costs extra. Some patrons linger to chat with the barista, but most down the contents of their cups in several sips and take their brioche in a napkin to go. Italy forgoes the trend of latte art and pour-overs in this economical process, instead favoring the staple stimulants of caffeine and sugar, because when done well, these things need no adornment.

Caffè sospeso is another Italian espresso tradition that's sure to keep growing. Buying a caffè sospeso slows down the mechanical process of most morning caffeination rituals: It requires people to consider that maybe they're not the only ones in need of a boost. The practice doesn't cost much, but it does a lot to transform a mindless routine into a hugely mindful gesture.

PHOTOGRAPH: PARKER FITZGERALD

Kinfolk's take on Julie's bedside table: Table Lamp by Arne Jacobsen. Mid-Century Nightstand by West Elm. Low Porcelain Bowl by Frances Palmer Pottery. No. 04 Bois de Balincourt Candle by Maison Louis Marie. Wooden Tray, Carafe and Glass by Muji. White Duvet by Schoolhouse Electric & Supply Co. Washed Waffle Blanket by Fog Linen. Belgian Linen Knife-Edge Pillow Cover by Restoration Hardware.

WORDS
JULIE BOUCHERAT

My Bedside Table:
The Editor

*The editor in chief of Milk Decoration
magazine in Paris discusses what she
likes to have at hand while slumbering.*

The bedside table is the link between my sleepy state of mind and my awake one, like a transitional piece of furniture. I sleep very close to the floor and the ceilings in my apartment are really high: I really enjoy the sensation of having a lot of space above me when I'm stretched out in bed.

I keep a tall pile of my favorite magazines on the floor. I like to organize my magazines like a precious, well-ordered collection in the living room, but I keep the issues I haven't read yet in my bedroom. I also always have a book next to my bed, even if I don't read every night. I'm currently reading *Psychologie Pour Les Créatifs: Survivre au Travail (Psychology for Creative People: Survive at Work)* by Frank Berzbach. It gives you keys and secrets to staying creative, even when you have to be creative on cue.

Often I'm in my bed, neither asleep nor awake, and suddenly I have a flash of inspiration or come up with a simple solution to a complex problem. I like that state of mind, and I always write those ideas in a notebook so I don't forget them the day after. In general, the answers you've been searching for seem to come when you're not looking for them.

On my bedside table I keep a white antique ceramic amphora with all sorts of things hidden inside, a nice little lamp from the French brand Moustache that is called "The Cave" and a beautiful white candle by the Dutch makers Tineke Beunders and Nathan Wierink from Ontwerpduo (I like scented candles too, especially ones by the Japanese brand Muji). I use moisturizers by French brands such as Avène, La Roche-Posay and Bioderma, and I also have a plant for oxygen: It's very important for me to have some life around.

I try to have a glass of water next to my bed, but I often forget: My mother used to say I'm like a camel because I never get thirsty. I don't drink wine in bed, but you can be sure I drink plenty of it in the evenings! My bedroom is personal, so when my friends come over we always hang out in the living room or kitchen, but we never go into the bedroom. My apartment might be messy, but my bedroom has to be a timeless, neutral space.

In France we like to live the Spanish way of life. We often start work late at 10:00 a.m. and then have a late dinner at 9:30 p.m. I like having a shower just before going to sleep at 1:00 a.m. because I really enjoy going to bed in my good-smelling linen sheets with a sensation of purity, as if I were in a little cloud. When I wake up, I don't stay in bed for long. Instead I prefer to get up quickly, open the window, feel the sun and air on my face, and let the day begin.

WORDS
WAI CHU & DANIEL SEARING

Unexpected Pairings

We asked two culinary connoisseurs to tell us about some unusual flavor combinations that have won them over.

Chocolate & Lime

Chocolate can be notoriously demanding when it comes to finding the right partner. Its bold flavor and velvety richness will easily obscure secondary ingredients. Lately it's been paired with everything from bacon and pickles to seaweed, but these fanciful combinations rarely bring out the best in themselves. Recently I tasted an even more unlikely duo: chocolate and lime. At first you might think that these two flavors would throw your palate completely off the mark (the sharp tartness of the lime versus the acrid bitterness of the dark chocolate). But when done properly, this combination is harmonious, even extraordinary. All of this came to light on a recent trip to Paris and a visit to one of the many artisanal chocolate shops in the city.

Tucked away in an alley in the busy, gritty Bastille district is La Manufacture de Chocolat. For chocolate lovers, this destination trumps even the Eiffel Tower. The sleek modern temple to cacao is the latest gem in the culinary empire of the French chef Alain Ducasse. Using meticulously sourced beans from around the world, he makes an impressive array of truffles, pralines and ganaches with a captivating blend of flavors.

My friend asked me to bring back some of Alain's signature confections. I opted for an assortment of 21 flavors that fitted squarely into my carry-on. We started with the simple ganache and immediately noticed the pure, unobstructed bittersweetness. Next we tasted the flavored truffles (coconut, mint, raspberry, pistachio) and all the flavors escalated with each bite. Finally, we tasted the lime and dark chocolate one and were astonished by the depth and balance of the flavors. The acidity of the lime cut through the astringency of the chocolate and, with just the right amount of sweetness, the tannins in the chocolate loosened enough to let in the soft floral quality of the lime.

To try this at home, soften a square of dark chocolate on a wafer in the oven and scoop a dollop of lime curd or marmalade on top. Enjoy with a respectable pinot noir or a glass of milk.

WAI CHU IS A NEW YORK–BASED CHEF, COOKING INSTRUCTOR, COOKBOOK AUTHOR AND FORMER OWNER OF EL EDEN CHOCOLATES.

ILLUSTRATION: KATRIN COETZER

Red Wine & Cola

Although we love both of these drinks in the United States, this combination sounds strange or distasteful to many. Maybe it's the aspirational nature of red wine appreciation clashing with the prosaic nature of cola. If you've ever had a sweet vermouth and soda though—a common drink in Europe—you might have noticed that it has some cola-like flavors: sweet, herbal and fizzy. (Did you know there is lavender in Coke?)

I first tried red wine and cola, also known as a *kalimotxo* (pronounced "cal-ee-MO-cho"), at my wine bar. It became a favorite pick-me-up during a long shift. I've long been fascinated by both the high—but also the low—end of drinking tradition. I'd heard about kalimotxo from friends who'd tried it

in Spain where it's been associated with the Basque region since the '70s, and was reminded of it by Anthony Bourdain when his show visited Uruguay. It's ideal to drink while watching European soccer on TV (which plays during the day in my time zone, so a lower-alcohol drink with caffeine and a Spanish vibe is a good fit). It's perfect at picnics or brunch too.

A kalimotxo is usually mixed in equal parts with plenty of ice. Enjoy it in a short or tall glass (or the bottom half of a soda bottle). I don't recommend using the cheapest wine you can get, but rather the best you can stand to mix with cola. Use a cola with real sugar if you can get it, such as Mexican Coke or Boylan's Cola.

Many enjoy the kalimotxo with a squeeze of citrus. Some like to add a splash

of fruit or anise liqueur for flavor, and a dash of Fernet isn't a bad idea either. I like a little (or a lot) of bourbon in mine, which I call a kali-bro-txo. Cut yourself off after a couple of those.

Because it's rich, sweet and high in acid, it goes well with standard sports-fan fare such as pepperoni pizza, buffalo wings and all salty snacks, but don't be afraid to go upscale by pairing it with Spanish chorizo, a Catalan goat's milk cheese called Garrotxa or tapas such as patatas bravas. And it's heaven with a hamburger: truly the best of both worlds.

DAN SEARING IS A SPIRIT SPECIALIST WITH THE COUNTRY VINTNER, CO-OWNER OF ROOM 11, AUTHOR OF *THE PUNCH BOWL* AND A MEMBER OF THE D.C. CRAFT BARTENDERS GUILD.

PHOTOGRAPH: ALICE GAO; PROP STYLING: KATE S. JORDAN; FOOD STYLING: DIANA YEN

The Lunch Box: Leftover Turkey Sandwich with Cranberry Chutney

No need to be bored by leftovers—this variation on the turkey sandwich will make you anxious for your lunch hour to arrive. Cranberry sauce reimagined into spiced chutney sets this sandwich off with a sweet and savory note while the Brie adds a creamy finish.

FOR THE SPICED CRANBERRY CHUTNEY
2 tablespoons (30 milliliters) extra-virgin olive oil
4 shallots, peeled and diced
1 garlic clove, minced
1 teaspoon fresh ginger, peeled and minced
¼ teaspoon salt
¼ teaspoon dried red pepper flakes
1 cup (240 milliliters) prepared cranberry sauce

FOR THE SANDWICH
Dijon mustard
2 slices sourdough bread
¼ cup (10 grams) lightly packed sliced radicchio
3 ounces (85 grams) sliced roasted turkey
2 ounces (55 grams) sliced Brie

FOR THE CRANBERRY CHUTNEY: Heat the oil in a medium-size saucepan over medium-low heat. Add the shallots, garlic, ginger, salt and dried red pepper flakes and cook, stirring occasionally, until the shallots soften and become translucent, about 5 minutes. Stir in the cranberry sauce and increase the heat to medium-high until simmering. Reduce the heat to low and simmer 2 to 3 minutes to allow the flavors to come together. Let cool, and then taste to adjust the seasoning. The chutney will keep in the refrigerator for up to 5 days.

FOR THE SANDWICH: Spread a thin layer of mustard on the bottom of a bread slice, followed by the radicchio, turkey and cheese. Spread a thick layer of cranberry chutney on the remaining bread slice and assemble to make a sandwich.

WORDS
AMY WOODROFFE

Leaders of the Pack

Yukigassen (which translates to "snow battle" in Japanese) is a professional snowball-fighting match that involves the frosty slaughter between two teams of seven on a field of snow.

When everything accumulates a healthy layer of snow, it's only natural to smoosh a handful of the stuff into the vague semblance of a ball and hurl it at a friend. Call it child's play, intuition or old-fashioned fun. Or replace its spontaneous nature with a set of meticulous guidelines and call it *yukigassen*.

With the goal of grabbing the other team's pennant at the opposite end of the field or tagging opponents out via a clump of flying snow, the game borrows elements from dodgeball and capture the flag: If you're struck by a snowball then you're toast, and if your team's flag is captured then your whole team is toast. Each nine-minute match is divided into three grueling sets that are won by either having the most players left when the whistle blows or by seizing the opponents' flag. The team that wins the most sets is crowned the victor. Armed with speed, agility and purpose-built Asics helmets, each team is protected from the snowy onslaught by seven shields spaced across the field. The game can be played using two methods: an offensive style where the bravest player sprints to the center shield for the best chance to steal the flag, or a defensive style where teammates lob their icy arsenal from the safety of the back shields and pick off their enemies one by one.

Invented by the people of Sōbetsu, Japan, to improve the local economy during their wintry slow season, yukigassen is not a simple backyard snowball fight where getting snow lodged in your long johns is the worst that can happen: Players must defend their entire team's honor as they tread the thin, icy road to the world championship.

The first yukigassen competition took place in the shadow of the grumbling Mt. Shōwa-shinzan volcano in February of 1989, where 70 Japanese teams competed while being cheered on by some 7,000 fans. The game soon caught on in snowy locations the world over with the United States, Canada, Russia, Norway, Finland, Belgium, Holland, Sweden and even Australia forming their own yukigassen organizations. Today more than 25,000 international enthusiasts gather each year beneath the volcano for the Holy Grail of snowball fights: the annual Shōwa-shinzan International Yukigassen.

The sport has been artfully structured and is balanced by rules that keep everyone in check. For example, even though the players are surrounded by veritable white gunpowder, you won't see anyone sloppily scooping up fresh ammunition on the field for fear of being eliminated. According to the official "Laws of the Game" rulebook, yukigassen competitors must prepare their limit of 270 icy grenades using a snowball machine and have each vessel approved by the judges prior to every match. Far more serious than the popsicle mold it resembles, the snowball machine's output determines much of a team's fate—if operated poorly it will produce off-center, decompressed snowballs that are about as useful as throwing soup. However, through correct use and pro finishing touches, it will yield a mighty inventory of beautifully ruthless spheres.

During the battle, the prepared snowballs must be stashed at the back line and only rolled or passed by hand to the forwards, who then proceed to unleash the fury. Two throwing techniques dominate the game: The fatal fastball claims anyone exposed, and the well-aimed lob is the surprise attack for those taking shelter. There's no squabbling about whether or not you were struck either, as the scrupulous eye of the impartial referee is always watching you.

There's much to love about yukigassen: It's full of strategy, skill, sportsmanship and a bunch of snowballs. You may not be ready to join the merciless blitz professionally, but by taking a few pointers from the experts, you could elevate this season's humble snow barrage.

WORDS
DIANA YEN

Cooking with Conifers

Pine needles have many uses beyond holiday decor. They taste mighty fine in baking, roasting and cocktails too.

Pine needles are more than just the leaves of the decorative trees that sit in our living rooms during the holidays: They are edible and have a minty fresh flavor that gives a distinctive twist to many seasonal drinks and dishes.

ROASTING: When you next make a roast, try lining the pan with a bed of pine branches and place the meat on top. It'll create an aroma that brightens the dish.

SHORTBREAD COOKIES: Fold a couple of tablespoons of finely chopped needles into some basic shortbread cookie dough before continuing the normal baking process.

SKILLET-ROASTED POTATOES: Scatter a handful of needles, halved potatoes and salt in an oiled cast-iron pan. Roast at 425°F (220°C) until the potatoes are tender and crispy, about 30 to 40 minutes.

SIMPLE SYRUP: Stir together ½ cup of water and ½ cup of sugar in a saucepan until it boils. Remove from the heat and add ½ cup of chopped needles. Let the mixture steep for an hour, then strain and let cool. Use in cocktails instead of basic sugar syrup.

SALT RUB: Combine equal parts pine needles and coarse salt, and pulse in a food processor. Use as a rub for your favorite meats or include it in a brine.

WORDS
STEPHANIE ROSENBAUM KLASSEN

In Defense of Fruitcake

Often banished to the depths of pantries or subtly spat into napkins, this holiday monstrosity has a reputation-saving background.

Forget the sugar-sparkled gingerbread cookies, the swirly candy canes and even the Hanukkah gelt. This holiday season, it's time to reclaim fruitcake.

Real fruitcake, that is, not its crassly commercial sibling, reeking of fake rum flavoring and roughly studded with molar-shattering hunks of candied pineapple and neon-green cherries. Pitched against the glamour and ease of fluffy triple-tier cake mixes, the lure of elegant French-style patisserie and the juggernaut of salted-caramel bacon super-chocolate everything, how could the fruitcake—a gentle cello overwhelmed by a full brass band—ever possibly compete?

Before it became the holiday gift-giving equivalent of a three-pack of tube socks, fruitcake had a long and noble history. Its origins date back to at least the late Middle Ages, when newly burgeoning trade routes along the Mediterranean and beyond brought back delicious, costly things: dried and candied fruits, fragrant spices, citrus and almonds... The lavish result? Fruitcake.

In the United Kingdom, no royal wedding was—or still is—complete without the grandest and most labor-intensive of cakes. Rich, dense and long-lasting, fruitcake was a very handy thing to have around the castle, especially if you were feeding hundreds of royal subjects or impressing visiting lords and ladies for weeks on end. And it extends beyond the Brits: In Italy, sticky Tuscan panforte and its cousin, Bologna's glossy fruit-topped *certosino* cake, still bear the flavor of medieval mincemeat redolent with the wares of Venetian spice traders.

These days if you really want to find a fruitcake worth eating, skip the mail-order monasteries. Instead, search out a Caribbean restaurant, a Jamaican jerk joint or a Trinidadian café and beg for "black cake." Born in the West Indies as a remnant of British colonial rule, black cake is a close cousin of both fruitcake and plum pudding and is nearly ebony-black with a dense and velvety texture.

The spirit of choice in black cake is dark rum, which makes sense considering that rum is distilled from the islands' plentiful sugar plantations. Dried and candied fruits are soaked for months in rum and port, and the finished cake is drizzled daily or weekly with *even more rum* to keep it moist until serving. Offering the sneaky kick of a cocktail cloaked in the spicy-sweet innocence of dessert, there's no better indulgence at the year's end than toasting friends with a forkful of these cakes, rich in flavor and history.

PHOTOGRAPH: RAHEL WEISS

WORDS
DAVID COGGINS

All Wound Up

———

*When the right scarf finds the
right neck, it can add more to its
owner's character than warmth.*

My family feels very strongly about
scarves. They wear them devotedly and
generously give them to one another, but
then "borrow" them back, sometimes
without asking and for extended periods.
It's not uncommon for my dad to say
to my sister, "That's a great scarf—is it
mine?" I shake my head, but I understand

the connection people have to scarves.
After all, you develop an attachment to
something you wear every day. A good
scarf does more than keep us warm: It
shows the world a hint of personality,
a flash of color, a blaze of pattern and a
sense of style. While the rest of your wardrobe rotates, the perfect scarf captures

your feelings for the season. Many years ago as a student in Paris, as the weather turned cooler I began to consider what scarf to wear. I didn't want to look too eager and be the first person strolling down the Rue du Bac in advance of the season, but I needn't have worried. On the first cool day, men, women and children were all draped in a brilliant array of scarves. Nonchalantly wrapped, brightly colored, inevitably elegant: This was accessorizing as high expression. A scarf reflects the wearer's worldview. It can be playful or discreet, whimsical or audacious, but it should never seem as if you stared in the mirror and retied it endlessly. It should look personal, even adored, but at the same time like you've forgotten all about it. Ultimately, scarves offer a change of pace from the habit of dressing. It's a well-earned point of interest, something optical, something warm, something close to the heart of anybody who cares about style. Just ask a Parisian.

Winter

PHOTOGRAPHS
AARON TILLEY

SET DESIGN
KYLE BEAN

FOOD STYLING
IAIN GRAHAM

The Hunger Games

Chocolate dominoes, shortbread Jenga and Turkish delight checkers—who says playing with your food shouldn't be creative?

INTERVIEW
GAIL O'HARA

PHOTOGRAPHS
ANDERS SCHØNNEMANN

A Day in the Life: Mikkel Karstad

Some folks seem to get that work-play-swim-life balance just right. Copenhagen chef, cookbook author, daily swimmer and father of four Mikkel Karstad is one of them. He explains how he keeps the different areas of his life working in harmony.

What kind of morning rituals do you have? — I swim in the sea every other morning. That's where I clear my mind and find peace. It gives me energy and makes me feel free, healthy and alone (in a good way). I'm around many people at work and at home so it's often very busy. It's important for me to have time alone, even just a half hour a day. I start work early, so my family is asleep when I leave. When I get to work, I drink coffee, eat a slice of rye bread with good cheese and then start working. I begin by baking bread and then I'll meet with the suppliers and check deliveries to make sure the quality of the produce coming in is high enough.

How does living near the water affect your lifestyle? — We use the water a lot for swimming, playing with the kids and sitting by the pier while eating dinner. My wife's dad has a sailboat, so we also go sailing. In the summer we spend a lot of time in Tisvildeleje, a coastal town that's very beautiful. The sea is an important part of our lives—I couldn't imagine not living near it!

How do you divide your time between work and play? — I go to work early so I can pick up the kids after school and spend time with them before dinner and homework. When they're asleep, I usually sit down with the computer and write recipes and work on different projects. When I'm with my wife and kids they're my number-one priority, then work and social life and time for myself. I've found a good balance.

What do you do for pleasure? — I spend time with my family, or I might spend a little time playing football with old friends. And if there's any time left, I spend it with good friends, making some nice food and drinking good wine.

What kind of family did you grow up in? — My parents got divorced when I was four, so I spent most of my childhood with my mother, which was very safe and supportive. She taught me to believe in myself and think independently, but I always knew there was support if I needed it. I left home at 17 and started working in restaurants— I spent a year in London and then worked and lived in Copenhagen.

When did you learn to cook? What are some early childhood memories of food? — I first learned about good homegrown ingredients and homemade food when I was a kid. I was inspired by my grandparents who grew vegetables and caught fish on Funen Island. My grandmother worked for many years as a *kogekone* (cook), so she was good at cooking like my mother. I never saw it as fine gastronomy—just lovely home-made food with good ingredients that were in season.

What kind of knowledge about food did you inherit from your family? — We used everything and never threw anything away. We made soup from the bones of fish and poultry and used all the parts of the vegetables. We didn't talk so much about sustainability in those days: It was just a natural part of daily life and "cheap" housekeeping.

Do your eating habits change at different times of day? — I try to eat a solid breakfast every day, and on weekends it's the most important meal because we're all home and have time to sit, eat and talk. Lunch is mostly snacking because we're usually busy at work. We attempt to have dinner with the kids, but they often have activities such as football and dance, so it's rare we're all at home. It's an important meal where we try to

sit together and chat while eating some good home cooking. On Sundays we also do a family dinner with my wife's family.

Please tell us about your children. — Oscar, 15, loves school. He's always played football but now is more into fitness and training. He also has a part-time job at a restaurant. Alma, 9, is happy about school and all her friends. She has gone to dance classes since she was 4 (modern funky jazz and hip-hop.) Konrad, 7, is very active, so he needs a little time to get used to school. He plays football, and I help coach his team. Viggo, 3, is the youngest and therefore probably extra-spoiled. He's a bit fussy, but I'm sure that will change. They don't eat everything, but they're curious to taste things and enjoy going to the forest to gather herbs, mushrooms, berries and other things. They have a healthy attitude toward food.

What kind of activities do you do with your children during the day? — We do homework and sports together, and then they help a bit in the kitchen. On weekends they often go off to play with their friends, but sometimes we go walking in the woods together looking for things we can forage: We find wild herbs in the spring, elderflower and rose hips in summer and berries, nuts and mushrooms in autumn.

What kinds of lessons or wisdom do you want to pass on to your children? — Use common sense in the way you treat other people, the way you eat and live, and the way you take care of each other and the earth.

You used to cook for the Danish parliament. What was that like? — It was a very big and exciting job: I was the head of 25 chefs and we had to make food for an awful lot of people with very different needs, 24 hours a day.

What kind of work are you doing these days? — I have my own company. I run the canteen at a law firm called Horten, where I offer breakfast, lunch and concierge service at the staff restaurant for 240 employees and their clients, along with my staff of four chefs in the kitchen. I also write about food for magazines and do food styling for advertising agencies, food companies and cookbooks.

Do you treat food differently at home than at work? — I cook using the same principles both at work and at home: I make easy, simple food focusing on local ingredients and produce that's in season and let the flavor of the ingredients shine through. It's simple, honest food that tastes great. Of course,

the difference is at work it's for 240 people and at home it's 6… but apart from that, it's the same.

The dishes featured on your blog, *We You They Ate*, and your cookbook, *Spis*, all use simple ingredients. Why do you choose to cook like this? — We have so many great ingredients around us—I like to keep my food simple so that the ingredients stand out… The food is transparent and honest.

Can you talk about the importance of presentation, plating and the beauty of food? — The first way you "eat" is with the eyes, so it's really important that the food looks pretty and appetizing. We should always know what's in the food and let it speak for itself. This is true whether you're serving food for guests or you're styling food for photos. I present and plate food in the same way I cook it and think about it.

What's the most important part of your day? What makes you feel at home? — When I have my family around me, it's both the most important part of my day and makes me feel at home.

Read Mikkel's recipe for Sole and Brussels Sprouts with Almonds, Tomato and Tarragon on the following pages.

SOLE AND BRUSSELS SPROUTS WITH ALMONDS, TOMATO AND TARRAGON

This recipe comes from Mikkel's cookbook, Spis (meaning "eat" in Danish), which focuses on simple ingredients. This fish dish can be served with potatoes, a basic salad, cooked greens or just good bread.

4 ½ tablespoons unsalted butter

1 shallot, thinly sliced

1 cup (240 milliliters) chicken stock
   or broth

⅓ cup (75 milliliters) dry white wine

7 ounces (200 grams) Brussels sprouts,
   trimmed and leaves separated

1 medium tomato, cored,
   seeded and chopped

⅓ cup (50 grams) toasted almonds,
   coarsely chopped

1 sprig tarragon, leaves coarsely chopped

Sea salt

4 skinless sole or plaice fillets

Freshly ground pepper

All-purpose flour

2 tablespoons extra-virgin olive oil

Melt ½ tablespoon of the butter over medium-low heat in a sauté pan. Add the shallot and sauté until soft and translucent, about 2 minutes. Pour in the stock and wine, increase the heat to medium-high and bring to a boil. Simmer until the volume is reduced by half, about 10 minutes. Strain the sauce through a sieve into a medium saucepan.

Return the sauce to medium-low heat and whisk in 2 tablespoons of the butter. (Do not boil after the butter is added or the sauce will separate.) Add the Brussels sprout leaves, tomato, almonds and tarragon and gently cook, stirring occasionally until warmed through and the leaves are slightly wilted, 2 to 3 minutes. Season with salt to taste.

Meanwhile, rinse the fish under cold water and pat dry. Season each fillet with salt and pepper, then turn them in the flour for a light, even coating.

In a sauté pan, heat 1 tablespoon of oil and 1 tablespoon of butter over medium-high heat until bubbly. Add 2 of the fillets and cook until golden brown and crisp, 2 to 3 minutes per side. Transfer the fish to a platter. Wipe out the pan and repeat to fry the 2 remaining fillets.

Pour the warm sauce and vegetables over the fish and serve immediately.

Recipe adapted from Mikkel Karstad's Spis (Lindhardt og Ringhof, 2014).

WORDS
JOHN STANLEY

PHOTOGRAPHS
MARK SANDERS

STYLING
ROSE FORDE

Duel Intentions

*With the rain beating against our windowpanes,
venturing inside for some physical recreation may be safer
than slipping on the sidewalk, even if it involves swords.*

To fence, you must don a particular uniform: a suite of clothes, actions and words collated from European traditions hundreds of years old. Originally, the art of swordsmanship was formally taught in order to allow men to duel whenever honor needed satisfying—though these face-offs usually ended when one side drew blood, rather than ending in death. Over time, fencing was taught more for sport than combat and became fashionable in an age of uncertainty and revolutions—American, Industrial and French—as something that spoke of an earlier, prouder time. The history and rituals of fencing have quietly resonated through the centuries. To start, you've almost certainly sparred with some fencing lingo at some point: The sport has gifted English some particularly sparkling words such as riposte, feint, parry, foible and lunge. The uniform hasn't changed much—the traditional garb was white to reveal blows from red-tipped swords, though hits are now often recorded electronically—but the wire masks were only introduced in the 18th century by French fencing masters. Before that courtly, blade-happy time, masks were often regarded with unease: Putting one on suggested you didn't regard your opponent as skilled enough to not accidentally hurt you when sparring, which was deemed insulting. Cut from murderous roots, it took another century or so for the various strands of European swordsmanship to cohere into a modern Olympic sport that still captures modern imaginations with potent notes of chivalric history and quick, bloody violence. In an age of global unease about the future and endless digital distractions, people seek things gone missing: romance, self-discipline, epic challenge. Now that people carry smartphones instead of swords, many thrill-seekers are turning back to this ancient art form. The lure of the blade never goes away.

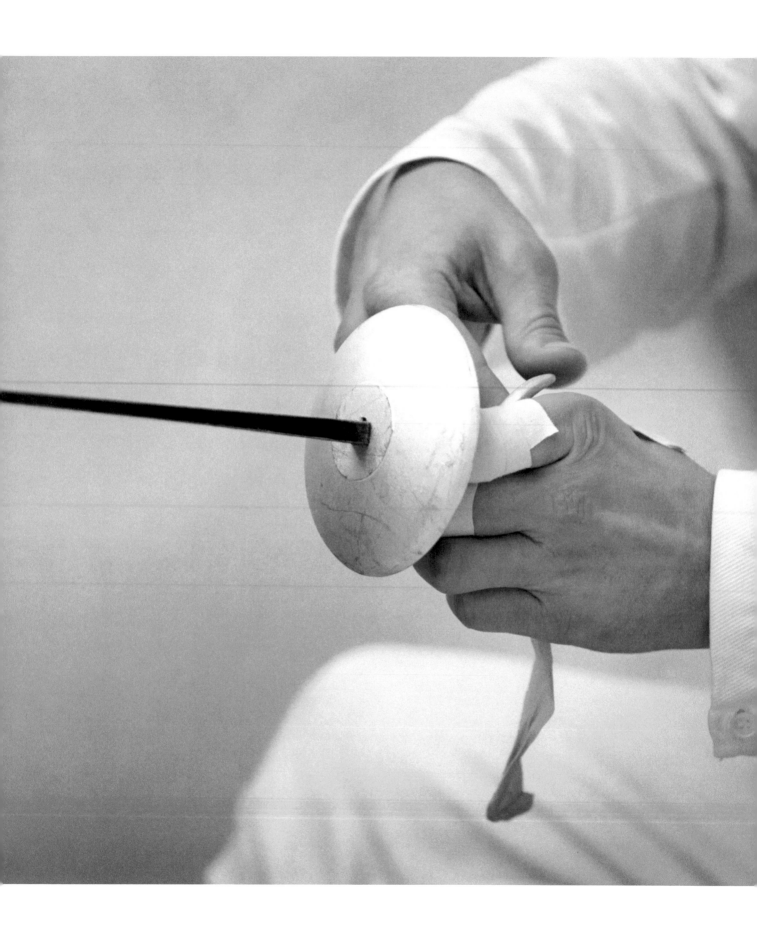

WORDS
JULIE POINTER

PHOTOGRAPHS
TRINETTE & CHRIS

The Solace of Soaking

*Nothing revitalizes tired bodies and minds more than
a morning spent bathing in healing mineral water.
Whether you choose to soak in a natural hot spring or sauna,
the looming steam rejuvenates more than your skin.*

The subtle indulgence of soaking enlivens the senses, opens the pores and soothes beyond the surface of the skin. Heat's fog invites us to sigh away our inner heaviness while calcified worries dissolve in the steam. They say time heals all wounds, but time is a luxury, and sometimes afflictions need a faster balm. Sweat, tears, the sea—all find their form in soaking where salty beads sting the eyes, slip down the nose, fall across lips. The pools purge tired bones and minds of ailing aches.

Entering a hot spring is complete surrender. The body does what it pleases—skin crinkles with time and goose bumps rise against the air. With nothing to hide behind, the human form becomes precisely what it is: a vessel of muscle, movement, matter and meaning. All forms are acceptable to water, every sharp elbow and battered knee. Here, impartiality reigns supreme.

The open air of a hot spring alarms naked skin at first. It's shocking, like ice on the neck on a summer's day. Something childlike takes over at the water's beckoning and we give way to buoyancy and slip into calm. Dipping our first toe into the pool reassures us that the vulnerability of bareness is well warranted, and the brief, awkward moments of revealing our unclad bodies are soon forgotten. Our timid nature and the ratio of warm to cold diminishes as our limbs descend. Warm water envelops us like an embrace—nothing could be more intimate against every inch of skin.

Our bodies spend their days dwelling between waking tension and sleeping peace. It's uncommon for them to reach equilibrium with our conscious mind, but in those rare respites when our intellect stops churning, we can begin to look, listen, feel, bask and relish in our immediate surroundings. In the seeming weightlessness of water, the mind forgets its faculties and experiences what it is to simply be.

WORDS
LIZ CLAYTON

PHOTOGRAPHS
HIDEAKI HAMADA

STYLING
MAMI OONISHI

How to Hibernate

Drafty rooms, lukewarm tea, wet socks: When the cold winds blow in, wouldn't it be nice to curl up into a fuzzy ball and snooze through winter? Humans may not be able to hibernate in the way some animals do, but we can find moments of brief respite from the season's chill.

So you're not cut out for winter. You're a victim of geography, caught in a stream of life's currents that has lodged you in between the rocks of an icy, unpredictable place that requires boots and shoveling. This season isn't your thing, and you'd live without it if all else within your heart wasn't stuck in this frosty town. But it would be easier—easier than moving, anyway—to sit this one out, wouldn't it? Just skip winter altogether? To return rejuvenated and amorous with the first crocus of spring and never once suffer the indignity of sticking cellophane to the windows, of guiltily lodging rock-salt crystals in the feet of innocent dogs?

We human beings don't traditionally hibernate, and we have our reasons. But the burly bear and the busy bee, the fat-tailed dwarf lemur and the operculate snail surely have good reasons that they do. Where they have slowed metabolisms, we have ramen. Where they may double their body fat for an eight-month stretch, we take the Hudson's Bay blanket out of the cedar chest. Where they snuggle in groups, we snuggle in groups only when socially acceptable. Perhaps, as it turns out, these creatures are onto something.

Hibernating animals simply have some things intrinsically figured out that humans don't. Try as we might to insulate ourselves from seasonal freezing and isolate ourselves from the disagreeable parts of daily living, there are only so many noise-canceling headphones and woolly mittens we can throw at the problem. For some of us, hibernation and escape are the same side of the coin, moments of relief that we in cities and towns strive toward in every season. But for animals, hibernation can be a true, emphatic departure from their surroundings. We can only hope to learn from them.

If a person is going to work up a speciesist envy toward those on the planet who fast-forward through winter, that person should have the facts—the first of which is that not all hibernation modes are created equal. From diapause to torpor, from wintering-over in a den to closing the lid on one's snail shell, it's different snoozes for different folks. Perhaps it's time to take a look at some of the big differences in the ways that species cheat winter.

BUGS: Many people hope the bugs they like least won't make it through the harsh conditions of winter. But for every hateful class of insects that survives, there's another friendly insect or two that also sleeps through the long winter's night, such as the ladybug and the honeybee. Many insects hibernate in a state called diapause, in

which they store up extra molecular needs for the power-down, engage in a little self-waterproofing and cease development and sexual activity. Insects may undergo diapauses naturally as part of their life cycle, or they may enter into the state as a response to stimuli like decreases in temperature or light. Awakening from diapause, many insects enact their equivalent of our well-rested morning stretches and sun salutations or, in the case of the Colorado potato beetle, lift themselves from their winter-long soil beds and march en masse to defoliate the nearest crop of potato plants.

BIRDS: Perhaps the species most commonly associated with migration, birds have few requirements by way of hibernation. After all, the next best thing to sleeping through an awful winter is flying far away to a warmer destination (if that's even your thing, which isn't true for all birds). But there's one odd birdie that nearly hibernates: the common poor-will, a stubby little bird from the nightjar family native to the North American west. The poorwill's version of hibernation is really a prolonged torpor, which is a state of low-power energy conservation by way of dropping its internal temperature—a phenomenon that vampire enthusiasts will already be well acquainted with. Unlike the predestined cycles or externally triggered causes of diapause, torpor states can be entered into voluntarily. Many birds and a few mammals do this daily, but what makes the poorwill unique is that it's able to spend several months with its body temperature throttled down to meet the cool temperatures around it. The poorwill's Hopi name is even "hölchko," meaning "the sleeping one."

BEARS: Oh, bears. These creatures have long occupied a mythologized, cozy and adorably curled-up place in our minds as the ultimate hibernators, but their status as "true" hibernators has been disputed. The definition of mammalian hibernation used to be characterized by a prolonged drop in body temperature—a practice the fat, fuzzy bear does not partake in. But now, thanks to the bear, hibernation has been redefined as a cold weather–driven reduction in metabolism concurrent with the absence of food. Or you may prefer to join those who refer to bear hibernation as "denning," which conjures up the idea of a very nice smoking jacket and leather-bound novel. That said, credit must be given to the temperature-drop hibernators—like your chipmunks, deer mice and ground squirrels—who not only drop to ambient body temperatures but also slow down their otherwise speedy hearts to a scant few beats per minute. For the rest of us, this would take lots and lots and lots of meditation.

LEMURS: And of course it wouldn't be fair to omit the lemur. The fat-tailed dwarf lemur, the only tropical mammal to hibernate, sticks itself into a tree hole for more than half of its Madagascar year, able to endure—and synchronize with—the incredible fluctuations in its environment. What's more peculiar is that the lemur's behavior isn't a dramatic response to temperature (it is warm, of course, in Madagascar) but rather a response to the dry season. If you were going to be thirsty for half the year, you'd probably find a tree hole too.

But what if we tried it? Truly tried it? What if a human in a typical habitat of, let's say, Columbus, Ohio, could hibernate? He or she might enter a series of cycles slowly building up—or down—to that magical retreat. We'd fatten up all summer at custard stands and begin gradually dialing down our heart rate and metabolism, seeking out the most well-insulated den possible, perhaps in a warm university furnace room, and cozy up for that long, dark journey until the beautiful day we can pop out into the light and eat up all the potatoes.

We can dream of such a day, yes. But our metabolisms haven't been set up for this because, evolutionarily speaking, they haven't needed to be. We're fairly new adopters of living in colder climes and have relied on culture and technology to step in where biological responses could have otherwise slowly formed. While the fat-tailed dwarf lemur naps parched in REM sleep, the human in Columbus instead has a stockpile of bottled water and craft beer. Where the ladybug, whose body involuntarily responds to light and cold, will retreat to some loose wood bark to sleep off her diapausal slowdown, the human in Columbus will take that same wood to stoke a fire, or use her iPad to order light boxes to stave off Seasonal Affective Disorder.

That said, for all those migrating humans who dream of all-inclusive Riviera escapes or flock in vehicular legion from Canada to Florida each winter, there are those among us who crave this time. The types who would endure the indignity of slush-soaked shoes for those quiet hours right after a heavy city snowfall. Those who eagerly await the appropriate time of year to unpack the Icelandic sweaters, to fill canisters with cocoa and to watch entire seasons of television unblinkingly. In these frosty conditions, we can revel in the very human ability to create not just warmth but the idea of coziness we've invented along with it. It's a feeling almost as sweet as that first coming alive day of spring, when you toss off your fleece-lined jacket and run hungry and euphoric into the world.

AN AUTHENTIC PRESENCE TO FOOD

———

We tend to either overthink or underthink our relationship with food, either compulsively documenting our dinner or disregarding it altogether by wolfing down salads at our desks. The beauty of eating lies in its ephemeral nature, and the process deserves to be distraction-free so we can enjoy those brief moments to their full potential.

This excerpt was adapted from "Authentic Presence to Food," an essay by Professor Deane Curtin that was originally published in Cooking, Eating, Thinking: Transformative Philosophies of Food *in 1992.*

Food is experienced only briefly. Yet far from being diminished in value because it's transient and contextual, its value is precisely that its "moment" comes and goes. To experience a raspberry fresh from the garden requires experiential knowledge of when to pick it, receptivity to the moment it is tasted and a timely appreciation of its flavors and textures. We must be fully present in the moment. If we're distracted, or use that moment for some other purpose, we will miss the experience. (Part of our fascination with the plastic mock-ups of food that Japanese restaurants set in their windows as advertisements is that, while they look somewhat like food, they lack an essential property of food: change.)

These observations serve to introduce the idea of an authentic presence to food. If we are to understand food in such a way that its flavor is not lost in abstractions, we must be willing to acknowledge our relations with it in such a way that they are not falsified by a theoretical bias for the abstract and the atemporal. We must draw out and highlight the appropriate and timely response to the present moment. We must learn to valorize the fleeting presence of *this*, here and now.

The Japanese philosopher Dōgen was deeply concerned with the relationship of food to the understanding of personhood and value. During a trip to China in 1223 to study in the great Buddhist monasteries, he met a temple cook who reproached him for thinking that the Buddhist path could be pursued only in the Meditation Hall, that enlightenment is separate from ordinary life. The path to self-understanding could be found as well, he urged, by forming a mindful relationship to ordinary things like food. When Dōgen returned to Japan, he found in Buddhist temples a lack of understanding of the relationship of food to enlightenment. He quickly moved to establish the *tenzo*, the temple cook, as one of the most important positions in the temple after the abbott.

Dōgen offers a suggestion on how to start thinking about authentic presence to food. He begins the *Fushuku-hampō* ("Mealtime Regulations"), a set of regulations for monks to help them realize their proper relations to food, by quoting from the *Vimalakirti Sutra*: "When one is identified with the food one eats, one is identified with the whole universe; when we are one with the whole universe, we are one with the food we eat." Dōgen understands our relations to food participatorily. We will see this, he thinks, if we focus on the everyday reality of our food. Instead of the common experience of a meal as a race one runs to get on to more "important" matters, Dōgen suggests we slow the mind to the point that we experience what literally becomes us through a temporal process of eating. By slowing the mind we can be instructed by food about the inherent temporality and relationality of life. Both the self and the food that becomes the self come together uniquely in each moment.

When Dōgen speaks about just being present to the rice he eats, he is not classifying this as a kind of experience, whether aesthetic or moral. He is not saying, "Appreciate the snowy whiteness of the rice," nor is he saying, "Recognize your duty to the food you eat." Such cognizing, even if necessary and appropriate at times, emphasizes separateness from the rice, which is being judged critically; interrelatedness is submerged. According to Dōgen, categories such as self versus other—the person eating versus the food eaten—are constructed only retrospectively. They are constructed as absolute categories only in reflection on the experience; they are not found in the moment of experience.

Instead of adopting a critical attitude, he is saying, "Be present to the experience; just eat the rice!" As [American author] Kim Chernin gives herself permission simply to eat her food and thereby discovers herself, so Dōgen is saying something very simple and ordinary like "Discover your ordinary self by just eating." Doing so mindfully

will be transformative in a way that leads to new aesthetic, ontological and ethical understandings.

Thomas Kasulis provides a phenomenological interpretation of Dōgen's use of the crucial Japanese phrase *genjōkōan*. Quoting [Heinrich] Dumoulin (1990), he glosses it as "This physical world, just as it is, is genuine, patent reality." Kasulis continues, "As directly experienced, impermanence is the 'presence of things as they are' (*genjōkōan*)" (Kasulis 1981, 84). Authentic presence to the rice one eats, then, can bring one into awareness of "genuine, patent reality" where reality is understood as the direct experience of impermanence.

The "knowledge" one comes to have through authentic presence to food is bodily and experiential. This is not conceptual knowledge prepared in advance and applied to the world. It is a kind of knowledge that comes to be for, and speaks authoritatively only to, the person or persons shaped definitively by a particular kind of experience.

Though Dōgen is asking that we experience food directly and hold off classifying it, there are numerous moral and aesthetic consequences that follow from acknowledging the mutual definition of self and food that occurs in mindful eating. Participatory self-definition may lead to living economically. If food is not the possession of an autonomous agent, if we understand ourselves to be defined partially by our relations to other human beings and to non human beings, food becomes something to be consumed with others in mind. As Dōgen points out, "From both the rational and practical outlook, one should try never to waste a single grain of rice at mealtimes; the whole universe is completely identified with the meal."

There is the illness of the anorexic who starves herself in a tragic attempt to achieve nonbodily purity. But there is also the healthful response to food that comes from taking only what one needs, and from eating with others in mind. Such an authentic presence to food cultivates the idea that eating is an act *in relation* to others: *This* grain of rice here and now is irreplaceable.

Furthermore, one may come to see oneself as functioning most healthfully within a specific context, for example, by coming to understand that some foods are appropriate to that context, and just as importantly, that other foods are not. When the Japanese see themselves as defined in an important way by being a "rice culture," this says something about what it means—spiritually, culturally and economically—to be Japanese. There is a focus on and a respect for a particular food that comes through exclusion as well as from inclusion, a focus that is lost in culture-hopping visits to the latest "ethnic" restaurant.

It is important to understand that the two food categories from which we normally operate both decontextualize food. "Food as technology" and "food as high art" can be regarded as two sides of the same view: Either food is cheap, fast and easily reproducible, or it is expensive, labor-intensive and difficult to reproduce. For this reason, "ethnic" food is now being advertised as the new chic form of high cuisine. But this "elevation" in status destroys its true character. In fact, it is neither "high" nor "low." What makes food "ethnic" is its deep connections to a specific cultural context. It is ordinary food in context.

[Writer and activist] Wendell Berry was thinking of the sense in which food exists most appropriately within a context when he said, "The pleasure of eating should be an extensive pleasure, not that of a mere gourmet." The gourmet judges food "objectively" whereas the cook has an "extensive" relation to food as ordinary and contextual. Ordinary experience is neither high nor low, neither exclusively moral nor aesthetic. It is healthy, everyday living.

Perhaps the most important result of authentic presence to food, though, is a sense of candor, transparency and openness to the food we eat; a simple willingness to face the reality of what we are willing to count as food; an "accurate consciousness of the lives and the world from which food comes" (Berry). To regard what we will *count* as food as a *choice* moves us from an attitude that treats food only as an object, to the beginnings of a food practice that gradually and relationally becomes a conscious expression of who we are. Such transparency allows us to appreciate the process by which plant foods become part of us physically, politically and spiritually. In particular, when we grant that eating is a moral issue, we can ask a question that has been disallowed by a culture that marginalizes food: Do we become violent literally (bodily) by being complicit in acts of violence done on our behalf to produce what we choose to count as food?

In summary, authentic presence to food is the direct experience of impermanence, of the physical world as "genuine, patent reality." It gives focus to our participatory relations with food and includes a way of understanding ourselves, an attitude toward food and a way of acting.

An adapted excerpt from "Authentic Presence to Food," Deane W. Curtin, *Cooking, Eating, Thinking: Transformative Philosophies of Food*, © 1992 by Indiana University Press. Reprinted with permission of Indiana University Press.

AN INTERVIEW WITH DEANE CURTIN

―――――

A lot has changed since Professor Deane Curtin wrote the preceding essay in 1992. He focused on the concept of mindful eating, something that has been pulled to two extremes in the modern day: those who willingly eat processed food and those who only eat organic. In a society where everyone documents lunch every day, can we make the most of our culinary moment? We asked Deane a few questions about the methods we can use to connect with our meals.

CAN YOU TELL US ABOUT HOW YOU WERE BROUGHT UP IN RELATION TO FOOD AND ITS VALUE?

I grew up in the '50s and '60s. My father cooked steak on the grill but was a complete stranger in the kitchen—I'm pretty sure he didn't know where the knives were. My mother was one of the '50s women who welcomed liberation from the daily demands of cooking from scratch. She adapted quite happily to the microwave and boil-in-the-bag corn. There's a mixed legacy here because many of our problematic relationships to food began then, but this revolution in the kitchen also allowed women that lived in a repressed age to begin imagining the freedom to do other things with their lives. My mother, for example, was trained as a professional photographer before she married my father—even when she was in her nineties she was happiest out in nature with her camera. The trade-off she made in the kitchen allowed her to have a life in which she could see her own place in the world.

HOW HAS OUR RELATIONSHIP TOWARD FOOD CHANGED SINCE THE EARLY '90s?

There's so much that seems hopeful. We now see food in the broader contexts of health, the environment, our relationships to non-humans and social justice. Food is an indicator of how we're doing on this planet. It requires us to see things as interconnected. When I teach environmental philosophy, I always begin the semester with one of the environmental footprint quizzes that are available online. They provide a quick picture of how we're doing both individually and as a culture. The conclusion of the quiz is an answer to the question, "If everyone lived with your environmental footprint, how many planet earths would there need to be?" I tend to be suspicious of an answer of less than about 2.5 from an American student (or from myself, despite my best efforts), and I've had students who report a score of 24 planet earths. By contrast, a few years ago I did a series of public talks in Peru to audiences numbering in the thousands. I asked them to do the quiz as I started to speak. I never received an answer above one world. If only as a matter of courtesy to the rest of the world, we need to become ever more aware of our food choices. As Americans, we sit on top of an unacknowledged pile of economic and environmental privilege that cannot continue. Our food choices are at the center of these issues.

IF YOU WERE GIVEN THE OPPORTUNITY TO REWRITE THE CHAPTER "AUTHENTIC PRESENCE TO FOOD" IN THE MODERN DAY, IS THERE ANYTHING THAT YOU WOULD CHANGE?

Actually, I can still stand to read it after all these years! My experience has deepened, but I still recognize myself in those words. Before I coedited *Cooking, Eating, Thinking* with my colleague Lisa Heldke, I'd lived in Japan for a year. I love a culture in which a single perfectly grown apple can be a gift to one's esteemed hosts. My students brought crickets to class just so we could listen to their sounds, and they took me moon-gazing beside a lake in Kyoto. This was the beginning of a slow process of realizing that "home" is not some exotic place I had yet to discover. It's any place where one is actually present. Food can be a touchstone for real presence just because it's so often dismissed as unimportant. One "refills the tank" so other important things can happen. But in truth, we are what we eat. When I travel with students, no matter what the official theme of the course, food appears at the core. Whether it's the Slow Food Movement in Italy, open-air markets in Peru (where there really are dozens of varieties of potatoes) or the culture of street food in India, food is always

an opening to what's really happening. So I don't think that the "Authentic Presence to Food" chapter would be that different today. I've only become more confident that real spiritual presence in the world is deeply practical, and much needed.

HAVE WE GOTTEN CARRIED AWAY AS A CULTURE ABOUT FOOD?

Of course. Food shouldn't become a fetish. I feel comfortable in cultures where food may be important, but it's just a normal part of a rich, diverse life. It's good in so many ways to make time in our lives for food, from health to family, friends and the environment. Awareness of interconnectedness is awareness of things as they really are.

HOW DO YOU VIEW BIG FOOD VERSUS LITTLE FOOD? GENETICALLY MODIFIED VERSUS ORGANIC? PROCESSED VERSUS FRESH?

Since the publication of *Cooking, Eating, Thinking: Transformative Philosophies of Food*, I've spent a lot of time in India, much of it in poor communities struggling to regain control over their local environmental economies. I've seen firsthand what happens when multinationals arrive and traditional systems of food security are disrupted overnight as farmers have no choice but to produce genetically modified organisms as export crops. But there's so much to learn from these traditional food economies. A couple of years ago I was walking through an Indian street with an Indian friend. He pointed out that the street-market tradition makes fresh food available to everybody: Wealthy people shop in the morning when the food is freshest and sold at the highest prices, but the poorer folks shop in the evenings since prices go down through the day. The least fresh food has been out of the ground for only a few hours. Brilliant. Fresh organic food is still too often an economic luxury in the United States. I would hope that in the coming years our tax subsidies shift away from factory farms and toward support for food for all that is both good for us and good for the environment.

IS OUR INCREASING AWARENESS ABOUT WHERE FOOD COMES FROM HELPING US BECOME A HEALTHIER SOCIETY?

I think the information printed on food packages should be expanded to include place of origin, how it was produced, the date it was harvested and so on. If we can require information on calories, why can't we also include information on the context from which the food came? In a capitalist economy, this information should be part of a consumer's right to know.

WHAT OTHER ACADEMICS, AUTHORS, BOOKS OR PAPERS WOULD YOU RECOMMEND US READING?

I still recommend Dōgen's essay "Instructions for the Tenzo." Take your time with it and let it sink in. It's available in several collections, including *Moon in a Dewdrop*. Carol Adams' book *The Sexual Politics of Meat*, originally published in 1990, was and is a revolutionary document: It's about the ways gender is constructed around concepts of food. My colleague Lisa Heldke has been a major figure in drawing philosophical attention to food. Her "The Unexamined Meal Is Not Worth Eating" (published in *Food, Culture and Society*, 2006) is a good place to start. Being present to food should invite us to reexamine what we think we know about other animals. I particularly like Marc Bekoff's books on animal intelligence and emotions, such as *Animals Matter*, cowritten with Jane Goodall. Frans de Waal's work on morality in nonhuman animals is also fascinating, for example *The Bonobo and the Atheist*.

YOU WROTE ABOUT HOW FOOD IS SOMETHING EXPERIENCED BRIEFLY. WHY DO YOU THINK MANY PEOPLE IN CURRENT SOCIETY ARE CONSTANTLY TAKING PHOTOS OF THEIR FOOD AND SHARING THEM WITH OTHERS? IS THIS A GOOD OR A BAD THING?

Good question. I've wondered what's really going on when people post photos of their meals while the meal is there, waiting on the table. It might reflect a genuine desire to be with others who aren't physically present. I'm open to the idea that community is evolving. It's not just defined by physical proximity anymore. But the nature of a photograph is to cut off a living, evolving process. It stops the conversation. There's obviously something troubling if social media posts become more real than the experience itself.

ANY ADVICE FOR STAYING TRUE TO THE EATING-IN-THE-PRESENT ETHOS IN THE MODERN DAY?

Eating in the present is an ongoing practice. Practices involve time. We get better at them by not just thinking abstract truths, but by engaging reflectively in our lives. Like the footprint quiz, mindfulness about food is an indicator of who we are and where we are.

YOU ALSO SPOKE OF "FOOD AS HIGH ART" AND "FOOD AS TECHNOLOGY." IT NOW SEEMS WE HAVE TWO EXTREMES WITH LITTLE MIDDLE GROUND. IS THERE ANY WAY THIS CAN BE RECONCILED?

I think that's right. We have extraordinary, fresh, healthy, expensive food for the few and what appears to be cheap, tax-subsidized manufactured food for the many. This system can't last much longer. Today's young people will have to fight to find their places in a world of almost 10 billion people. Both Bangladesh and Wall Street will experience the tides of global climate change as the oceans rise. These inevitable forces indicate that we desperately need to find a new center. I find hope in the real changes that have occurred since the early '90s. Change happens slowly on issues that run this deep. Most people aren't open to transforming their attitudes toward food by being attacked or coerced. Real change has happened, and we need to keep raising these issues, but I also have faith in generational change. On the other hand, I do wonder how much time we have. Things will change because we have no choice. The question is whether these changes in a crowded world will come collaboratively or through conflict.

Professor Deane Curtin teaches philosophy, ethics, environmental studies and community development at Gustavus Adolphus College in Minnesota.

RECIPES & WORDS
DIANA YEN

PHOTOGRAPHS
ALICE GAO

PROP STYLING
KATE S. JORDAN

The Cookie Collective

Team baking can be a tasty experience: Tray after tray of holiday-scented goods spill out of a single oven, often never making it to the decorating station in one piece. We offer up three delectable recipes to get you started and outline how to operate an all-out cookie-making day.

Cookies are everyone's childhood sweet spot. Growing up, I remember cookie baking was a full weekend event. It can be hard to maintain traditions when you live in the city or away from your family though, so a few years ago I began hosting a winter cookie-baking day.

My friends send me their recipes, I pick up all the ingredients and we spend the afternoon drinking hot apple cider and mulled wine while making treats to either gift to others or scoff ourselves. I'm a little bit of a cookie curator, so I make sure that some are crumbly, some are chewy, some are chocolate, some are jam-filled… Sometimes we'll get through five-dozen batches! Nothing beats baking together in a warm, cozy kitchen filled with sweet and comforting smells.

I divide my house into different stations that we rotate around: First you make the dough, then send it to the rolling station where you have a rolling pin, flour and stacks of baking sheets, then they go into the oven, then to the cooling station, then the decorating area and finally a place where you can wrap and box them up. You can either follow one cookie from start to finish or have people working at the same station on multiple cookies. The trick with the timing is to make a few batches of cookie dough in advance so that people can get started when they walk in. (And keep your butter out at room temperature so it's always soft.)

The day starts out being organized and then gets really chaotic. When you only have one oven, it's kind of a mess and sometimes cookies burn, but there's always someone willing to eat them. Anything tastes good with milk! You also start to get experimental, like mixing different leftover doughs together into one ultra-cookie. It's always going to taste good. Butter, sugar, flour: They're the basics that make every cookie delicious. Every bowl is licked clean—I barely have to wash.

I usually send wrapped-up cookies to my family in California, and I pass them out to people in the neighborhood, like the guy who picks up my mail: It's really nice to acknowledge people who you interact with every day. And for myself? I just eat the broken ones—that's often all that's left!

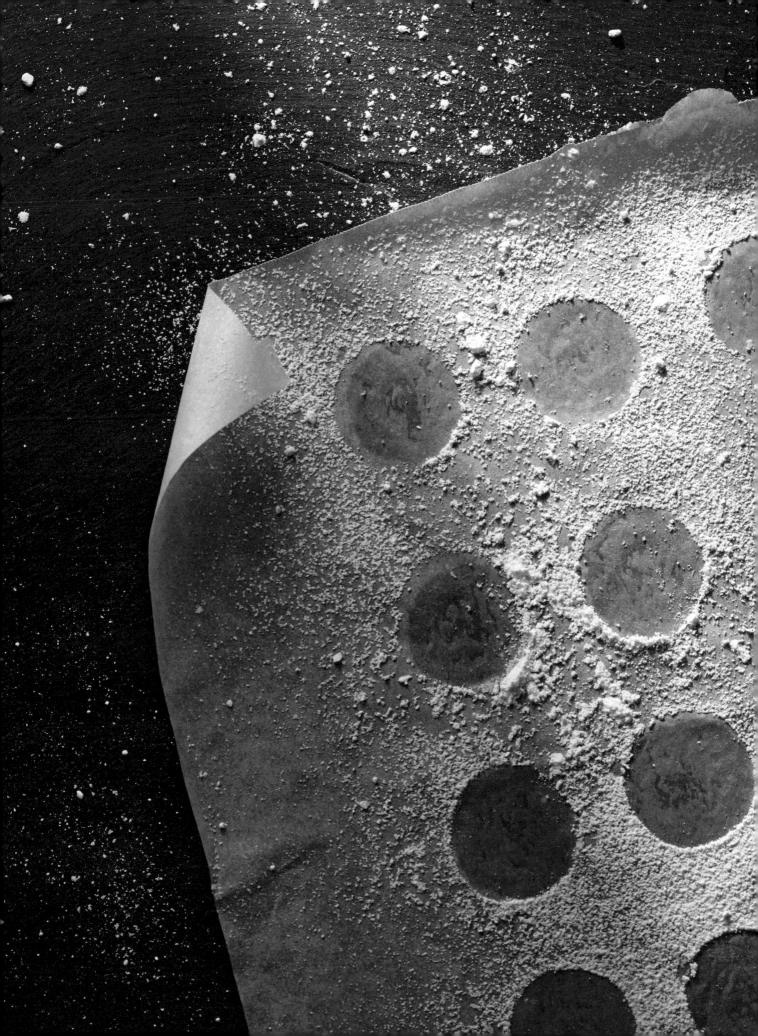

CHESTNUT COOKIE SANDWICHES
DIPPED IN DARK CHOCOLATE

FOR THE COOKIES

2 ⅔ cups (350 grams) all-purpose flour

¼ teaspoon salt

1 cup (2 sticks/225 grams) unsalted
   butter, softened

1 cup (185 grams) granulated sugar

1 large egg

2 teaspoons (10 milliliters) pure
   vanilla extract

FOR THE FILLING

⅔ cup (70 grams) powdered sugar

½ cup (1 stick/115 grams) unsalted
   butter, softened

½ cup (120 grams) chestnut puree*

½ teaspoon ground cinnamon

FOR THE CHOCOLATE GLAZE

8 ounces (225 grams) bittersweet dark
   chocolate (60 to 72 percent cacao),
   coarsely chopped

⅓ cup (40 grams) finely chopped
   toasted hazelnuts

FOR THE COOKIES

In a large bowl, whisk together the flour and salt.

In another bowl, using an electric mixer on medium speed, beat together the butter and sugar until pale and fluffy. Beat in the egg and vanilla. With the mixer on low speed, slowly add the flour mixture and mix just until a dough forms, stopping to scrape down the sides of the bowl as needed. Divide the dough between 2 sheets of plastic wrap and pat each into a disk. Wrap tightly and chill until firm, at least 1 hour.

Preheat the oven to 350°F (180°C). Line 2 baking sheets with parchment paper.

One at a time, roll out the dough to a ⅛-inch (3-millimeter) thickness on a lightly floured work surface. With a cookie cutter, cut 1.5-inch (4-centimeter) rounds and arrange them at least ½ inch (12 millimeters) apart on the prepared baking sheets. (Reform the dough scraps into a disk, wrap tightly and freeze for later use, if desired.) Bake until the edges are golden brown, 10 to 12 minutes. Cool on wire racks.

FOR THE FILLING

In a bowl, using an electric mixer on medium speed, beat together the powdered sugar and butter until pale and fluffy. Add the chestnut puree and cinnamon, and mix until smooth.

FOR THE CHOCOLATE GLAZE

Melt the chocolate in a small glass bowl set over a pot of gently simmering water, whisking occasionally, until just melted, smooth and glossy.

ASSEMBLE COOKIES

Place wire cooling racks over 2 baking sheets. Spread a thin layer of chestnut filling on half the cookies. Top with the remaining cookies. Dip half of each sandwich cookie into the warm chocolate and transfer to the racks to allow excess chocolate to drip off. Sprinkle the hazelnuts over the chocolate. Place the cookies in the refrigerator to set, about 20 minutes.

* Sweetened chestnut puree is often used in pastry and cake fillings or to make flavored creams. It's a smooth paste that will give a rich nutty flavor to your dishes.

PISTACHIO ROSEWATER SNOWBALL COOKIES

A traditional snowball cookie is crumbly, melts in your mouth and is lightly dusted with powdered sugar. They're also called butterballs, jumbles, Mexican wedding cookies, Italian wedding cookies, Russian tea cakes... everyone takes cultural credit for them! These ones have a delicate floral aroma and a bit of a Moroccan influence. They taste wonderful with mint tea.

1 cup (130 grams) unsalted shelled raw pistachios

2 cups plus 2 tablespoons (280 grams) all-purpose flour

½ teaspoon ground cardamom

¼ teaspoon salt

2 ¼ cups (200 grams) sifted powdered sugar

1 cup (2 sticks/225 grams) unsalted butter, softened

1 teaspoon rosewater

Preheat the oven to 350°F (180°C). Line 2 baking sheets with parchment paper.

Blanch the pistachios in boiling water for 1 minute. Drain, place in a clean kitchen towel and rub off the skins. Spread the pistachios in a small baking dish and roast in the middle of the oven until just dry, about 8 minutes. Set aside and let cool completely.

Place the cooled pistachios in a food processor and pulse until finely ground but not a paste. Transfer the pistachios to a medium bowl and whisk together with the flour, cardamom and salt.

In another bowl, using an electric mixer on medium speed, beat 1 cup (90 grams) of the powdered sugar with the butter until pale and fluffy. Add the rosewater and mix until combined. With the mixer on low speed, slowly add the flour mixture and mix just until a dough forms, stopping to scrape down the sides of the bowl as needed.

Roll the dough into 1.5-inch (4-centimeter) balls and arrange them at least 1 inch (2.5 centimeters) apart on the prepared baking sheets. Bake the cookies until they're golden on the bottom, about 20 minutes. When cool enough to handle but still warm, roll the cookies in the remaining powdered sugar. Let them cool on a wire rack.

MAPLE PECAN SHORTBREAD COOKIES

*Who doesn't love buttery pecans?
They have a warming southern flavor
and are such a nice way to sweeten
dough in a subtle way. This recipe
combines basic shortbread with hints
of other wintry flavors and is a bit
lighter than traditional shortbread.*

2 cups (260 grams) all-purpose flour

1 cup (120 grams) finely chopped pecans

¼ teaspoon salt

1 cup (2 sticks/225 grams) unsalted butter, softened

¼ cup (50 grams) light brown sugar

¼ cup (60 milliliters) maple syrup

1 large egg white, lightly beaten with
   1 tablespoon water

Coarse sanding or sparkling sugar, for rolling

In a large bowl, whisk together the flour, ½ cup (60 grams) of the pecans and the salt.

In another bowl, using an electric mixer on medium speed, beat together the butter, brown sugar and maple syrup until pale and fluffy. With the mixer on low speed, slowly add the flour mixture and mix just until a dough forms, stopping to scrape down the sides of the bowl as needed.

Divide the dough between 2 large sheets of plastic wrap and form each into a long log, about 1 ½ inches (4 centimeters) in diameter. Wrap tightly and chill until firm, at least 1 hour.

Preheat the oven to 350°F (180°C). Line 2 baking sheets with parchment paper.

Brush each log of dough with some of the beaten egg white and roll it in sanding sugar to coat evenly. Slice the logs into ½-inch-thick (12-millimeter) disks and arrange them at least 1 inch (2.5 centimeters) apart on the prepared baking sheets. Lightly brush the tops with the beaten egg and sprinkle with the remaining chopped pecans. Bake the cookies until they're lightly golden on the bottom, 10 to 14 minutes. Let them cool on wire racks.

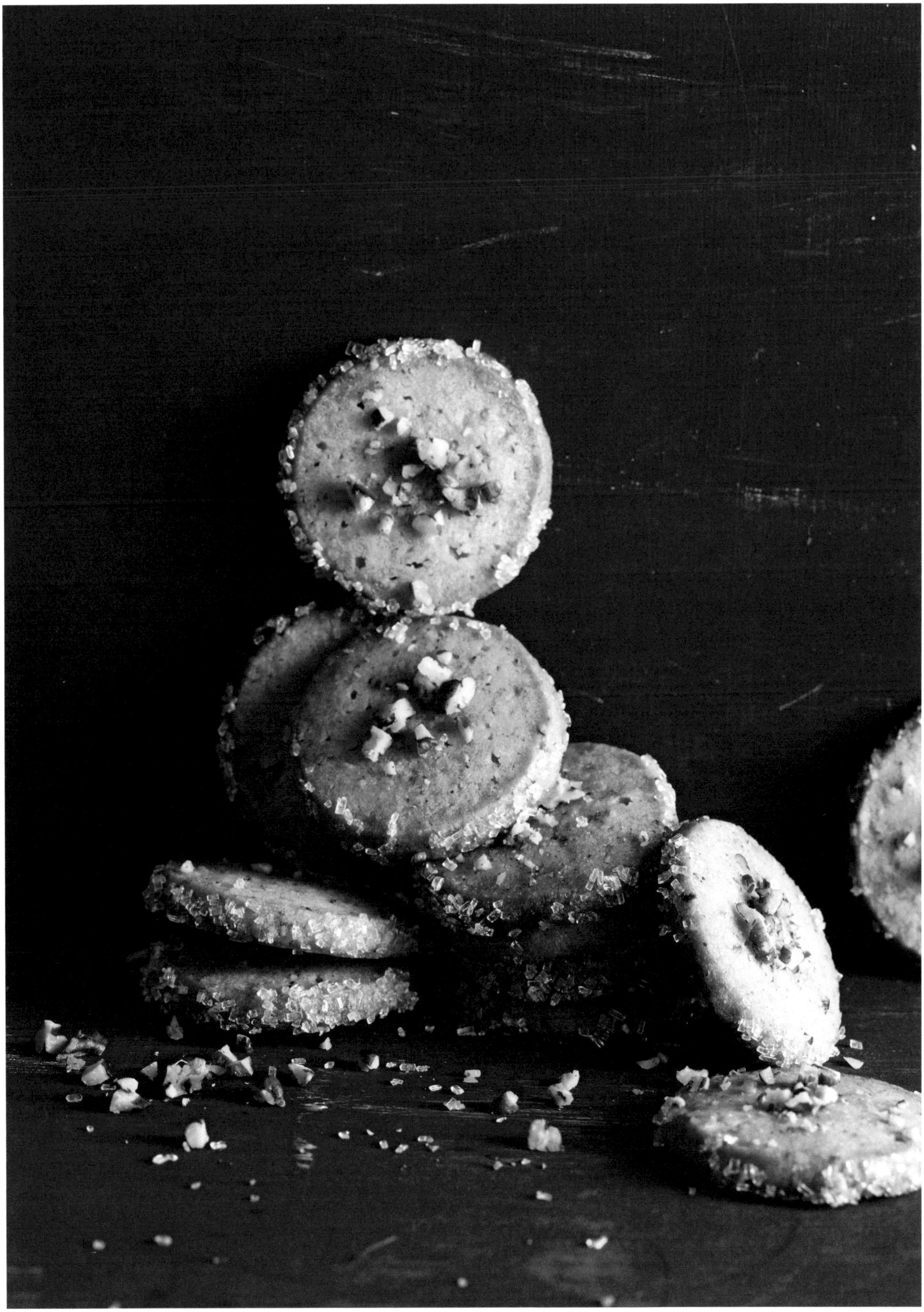

Peak

Ambition

*Brighton-based photographer Laurie Griffiths focuses his
lens on documenting the world's most indomitable expanses and
the thrill-seekers who attempt to conquer them.*

WHAT CONCEPTS ARE YOU INTERESTED IN EXPLORING THROUGH YOUR WORK?

My work is concerned with the impact of human beings on the landscape. I hope
they pose a contemporary challenge to the traditional understanding of the picturesque
and attempt to raise questions about how we commoditize and exploit natural spaces
in the pursuit of leisure and personal challenge.

WHY ARE WE ATTRACTED TO DESOLATE SNOW-COVERED LOCATIONS?

Frozen places are so hostile that their very presence becomes conspicuous. They are extraordinary spaces that offer a unique and incredible level of personal challenge that leaves me with a feeling that can't be replicated. Their beauty is undeniable, but there's always a sense of these environments' intrinsic threat: I guess that's their ultimate lure.

WHO WINS OUT IN A BATTLE OF THE ELEMENTS: HUMANS OR NATURE?

It's difficult for me to be overly critical of humans and their relationship to the environment
because I'm complicit in its demise. Ultimately, I expect there will be only one winner in
the struggle between humans and nature. Clearly we have the potential to wound and
inflict great harm on the world, but I expect we'll be the ultimate victims.

WHAT DOES THE SNOW MEAN TO YOU?

Learning to ski and the development of my photographic practice came at a poignant time in my life. My love of skiing has been part of a personal journey: I've never felt stronger, more complete or focused than when I'm 11,000 feet up a mountain. I found myself in the last place I would've thought to look, and I'm happy about it.

DEEP BLUE DAY (UNTITLED 12.6)
2012
Inkjet print in artist's frame
37 ⅝ x 40 ⅜ inches; 95.6 x 102.5 centimeters

WORDS
GEORGIA FRANCES KING

PHOTOGRAPHS
UTA BARTH

THE MEANING OF LIGHT

The daily rise and fall of the sun is one of the few reliable occurrences in our lives. Despite this simple cycle controlling the happenings of our planet, we don't pay much attention to sunlight's effect on our physical and mental health. And as some neuroscientists are beginning to discover, harnessing its radiant power could provide phenomenal benefits to our well-being.

Every day presents us with all kinds of decisions to make about our lifestyles, and there are plenty of self-diagnosis websites, new age books and mothers-in-law ready to indisputably instruct us on the correct choices we should make. In an attempt to better ourselves, we try to obey their mantras: We sleep eight hours a night; we opt for whole grains instead of white flour; we drag our reluctant bodies on a quick jog; we choose not to open the second bottle of cabernet. But what if there was a more vital factor affecting our health? One that predates gluten alternatives and spin classes?

For the past few billion years, the sun has reliably risen every morning and set every evening. Our bodies have therefore come to expect its daily spiral through the sky, and most of our biological systems work on the assumption that we'll follow along with its sunlight-based sequence. But now instead of waking with dawn, we have snooze buttons. Instead of dozing at dusk, we have Netflix.

Sunlight plays an intrinsic role in our lives and has a profound effect on the way we think and how our bodies function. Through its role guiding our circadian rhythms—the internal clocks that keep us regulated—sunlight can control everything from our sleeping habits to our wintertime melted cheese cravings. Regardless of the thought we put toward our well-being, it's becoming apparent that the sun could actually be the ironically inconspicuous guru we should be following.

Despite the sun's omnipresent nature, the effects of light on our mental and physical health are only just beginning to be examined. Two people who are working together to pioneer this exploration are an artist and a neuroscientist: Stephen Auger, a Santa Fe–based artist with an academic background in neuroscience who works at the intersection of science and art, and Dr. Benjamin Smarr, a doctor of neurobiology at UC Berkeley whose studies focus on the long-term effects of circadian rhythms on our physical and mental health. "A lot of people haven't heard of light's importance as 'a thing,' even though it seems very intuitive once you hear about it," Benjamin says. "I'd love to see much more attention paid to it. It's of absolutely central importance."

But how did we lose our connection to sunlight in the first place? Were we complicit in our demise into dimness?

SUNDIAL (07.5)
2007
Face-mounted color photographs
Overall: 30 x 57 ½ inches; 76 x 146 centimeters

Improving our relationship with the sun could help both our personal well-being and society overall

When Thomas Edison popularized the lightbulb some 135 years ago, he was unwittingly ending our close relationship with natural light. "The part of our DNA that responds to light is so primal," Stephen says. "It existed when we were a one-celled organism in the primordial ooze long before we became a human species." But now, thanks to the humble lightbulb, we can work graveyard shifts and salsa until dawn. As Stephen puts it, "We've objectified light." Convenience glowed brighter than our biological clocks, and we've been slowly letting them fall out of sync ever since.

In order to fathom light's consequence on our well-being, we first need to understand circadian rhythms. Our bodies are hungry for sunlight and have come to trust it to tell us when we should eat, socialize and sleep. "Your circadian rhythm is the body's anticipation of the 24-hour cycle of sunlight and darkness," Benjamin explains. "The sun has arced through the sky every 24 hours for all of life, so life forms have evolved to assume it's not just going to suddenly stop."

"Every single cell in your body has a clock that's trying to guess what time of day it is to get ahead of the game," he continues. "If my body knows that I get up and eat breakfast at 8 a.m. every day, then my liver, stomach and pancreas don't have to wait until there's food in my stomach to go, 'Oh shoot! We should be doing something about that.'" However, this preemptive response is only effective if we maintain a consistent routine based on the sun's movement— one that isn't influenced by impromptu midnight movie screenings and urgent deadlines. Technology and our desire to mingle have muted our biological reasoning, meaning our circadian rhythms' pleas for predictable schedules are often ignored. "People are generally dissociated with their connection to the environment," Stephen says. "And I wouldn't be the only person to say that a great deal of that has to do with light."

Thanks to everything from caffeine to night shifts, it's pretty easy to confuse our bodies' internal clocks, and this is especially common on the weekends. After five days of creating a semistructured morning routine, sometimes Saturday sleep-ins can leave us more tired than 6 a.m. starts. That feeling has a name: social jet lag. "It's a real thing and has a real effect, as your body is dumbly anticipating you'll get up at the same time as you did yesterday, because that's how it worked for the past four billion years," Benjamin says. This is also why Mondays can be such a drag—after two days of sleeping in, suddenly setting the alarm for dawn can shock our systems. "Your body's network has no mechanism to deal with alarm clocks or wanting to stay up to watch a movie," Benjamin says.

The act of taking care of ourselves via an awareness of sunlight's patterns is part of what Stephen and Benjamin call "sensory well-being." In addition to the other life choices we make to benefit our health, "Light is another piece of that puzzle we can now add to our lifestyles that's going to make a huge difference," Stephen says.

Improving our relationship with the sun could help both our personal well-being and society overall: If we learn how to look after ourselves through environmental adjustments, we'd free up the medical profession to concentrate on bigger problems. "Doctors shouldn't have to focus on the maintenance work—you wouldn't take your car to the mechanic every time it runs out of gas, right? That's a part of your daily maintenance," Benjamin explains. "But right now we don't really know a lot about how to maintain our bodies. And because we lack that maintenance, we therefore run into problems and need to go to the mechanic more often, which becomes a burden on the mechanics." By synchronizing ourselves with the sunlight's quirks, we may be able to help tune ourselves up the natural way.

... AND OF TIME (00.4)
2000
Color photographs in artist's frames
Overall: 35 x 90 inches; 89 x 228.5 centimeters

Here are some quick ways to fine-tune your light-related habits:

SET A ROUTINE

In order for our bodies to operate smoothly, all of our organs and systems are dependent on their clocks being wound to the same time. "They're not all able to look at each other's wristwatches though," Benjamin says. "You have to give them a routine to let them line up and coordinate." Getting up and going to bed at the same time every day allows our bodies to sync to a schedule, and we'd benefit even more by regulating the timing of meals too, like making oatmeal at the same time each morning.

SLEEP WITH A MASK

Sleeping eight hours per night is beneficial, but not if our bodies think it's daytime. Switching on the bathroom light or checking emails in a bout of insomnia might not be the biggest problem: The most disruptive factor may be ambient light pollution drifting in through the curtains. "Most bedrooms aren't well blacked-out, which often leaves them light enough that your brain registers the light all night long—especially in cities," Benjamin says. "Something as simple as wearing a sleeping mask can have a profound effect."

OBSERVE DAWN AND DUSK

While a lot is left to discover, it's beginning to appear that these times might be the most important parts of the day to be out and about: The light quality is changing rapidly and the direction of that change serves as a biological cue for whether it's early or late, thereby orienting our cells to wake up or wind down. "The subtle movement of light is an absolutely essential component to orient us to our circadian rhythms," Stephen says. This could be as simple as getting up 20 minutes earlier to walk the dog at dawn or having an excuse to snack on charcuterie while watching the sunset.

GET SOME REAL RAYS

They say that people who live in glass houses shouldn't throw stones, but they should throw open a window: Just like sunscreen helpfully blocks our skin from certain harmful light frequencies, the glass in windows deflects some other frequencies our bodies need to trigger biological responses. It's helpful that we don't burn while sitting in a sunlit office all day, but the fact we don't scorch is a clue that we're not getting all that the sun has to offer. It's best to bask during the times of day when dangerous ultra-violet wavelengths are less prevalent, such as the first and last couple hours of sunlight. "My doctor tells me I should lie out in the sun completely buck naked for 20 minutes a day. And I'm like, 'I like that doctor!'" Stephen says, laughing. In order to trigger vitamin D production, direct sunlight needs to shine on our bare, unprotected skin.

Circadian rhythms aside, vitamin D can also play a vital role in our sensory well-being. Our bodies naturally produce this small molecule when our skin absorbs certain helpful frequencies of ultraviolet light, causing a whole series of enzymatic responses in our cellular structure that help support a healthy immune system and balance our mood. Without its presence in our bodies, our defenses to nasty bugs weaken and our happiness also seems to nosedive.

So why natural light, and not just more lightbulbs? It's all to do with wavelengths: Just as we think of rainbows as color spectrums from violet to red, the same can be described in light wavelengths. The sun gives off white light made of all the wavelengths combined, but lightbulbs only give off a few (think of how a crystal swinging on someone's porch produces a rainbow when hit at the right angle, or Pink Floyd's *Dark Side of the Moon* album cover). Different wavelengths have different energies, so depending on the height of the sun in the

—

Every single cell in your body has a clock that's trying to guess what time it is to get ahead of the game sky, the rays that hit earth have different intensities—that's why it's a lot harder to get sunburned at 9 a.m. than at high noon. These wavelengths and intensities also have different effects on our bodies, from the tumor-causing overdoses of ultraviolet rays to the more positive ones that stimulate vitamin D production.

Experts are still trying to understand the complicated role vitamin D plays in our well-being, and mixed messages abound: A medical professional might tell us to wear 50+ sunscreen to protect us from cancer-triggering ultraviolet light and in the same breath instruct us to sit unprotected in the sun to kindle vitamin D production. "I don't want people to think if they hose themselves with vitamin D that all of their problems will be solved," Benjamin says. "It's one piece in a complex system that we're still understanding." Now that many of us spend our days within enclosed walls instead of outside in the wild, vitamin D deficiency has become fairly common. This is especially true in the winter when there are fewer sunlit hours in the day and therefore even less time to absorb the correct wavelengths we need to stimulate its production.

In the darker months, the combination of vitamin D deficiency and our disrupted circadian rhythms play a crucial part in Seasonal Affective Disorder, a.k.a. the aptly acronym-ed SAD. While some still consider this condition an imaginary excuse for not getting out of bed when it's dark, it is an actual emotional disorder brought on by chemical reactions in your body. It's often defined as when the natural traits that typify winter—the extra sleeping, the extra eating, the lack of desire to get out of the house and be social—are involuntarily taken to excess, which interferes with our ability to operate at our optimal level of mental health.

Our bodies anticipate seasons just like they do 24-hour days, so short instances of this stoic existence are a perfectly standard response to winter's lower light levels and dipping temperatures. For example, we're legitimately wired to crave carbs and fatty substances during the time leading up to the cold season to help us put on a nice layer of natural insulation—an evolved excuse for baking a second batch of mac and cheese. Except that where this was once a biological reaction that preempted a lack of winter produce, we now have all the food we hanker for available to us to consume year round.

"Historically it was great that my body craved cheese in October in anticipation of a cold snap," Benjamin says. "But here I am in Berkeley, in summer, where I can go out and spend a hundred dollars on cheddar and wolf it down, but that's probably not what my body intended." This is another example of how we've lost touch with what our bodies are geared to crave, and cues from sunlight might be one of the best natural ways to resolidify those missed connections.

The best ways to ward off the winter blues and be kind to your sensory well-being are the same year round: Set a routine to keep your circadian rhythms ticking, try to be outside with your skin exposed during daylight hours for as long as your frosty epidermis can bear it, and don't always reach for the wheel of Brie when the slightest cheese craving gurgles within you (only give in on some days).

But often the people most affected by SAD live in areas where they don't have the choice to bask in the sun, even if they wanted to. For the residents of the world's northernmost communities who don't experience a sunrise for months during winter, or night-shift workers who have to be awake during nocturnal hours, no amount of positivity and goodwill can tilt the earth on its axis to grab some more rays. Without normal hours of natural light, how can these populations possibly set any semblance of a steady circadian rhythm or produce enough vitamin D to stay healthy?

That's where artificial light starts to shine. Through a project that fuses art with science, Stephen has helped create an artificial light with the ability to replicate the movement of specific wavelengths of sunlight, potentially opening up a whole can of glowing worms for light-starved people around the world.

The technology was invented as part of *The Twilight Array*, an art exhibition that will take place at Gary Snyder Gallery in New York City this winter. For this project, Stephen collaborated with many esteemed experts (including neurobiologist Dr. Margaret Livingstone, founder of the Livingstone Lab at Harvard University and author of *Vision and Art: The Biology of Seeing*) to create a series of works that explore the subtleties of twilight perception. His paintings will be illuminated by a light that replicates the movement and wavelengths of twilight, sending the viewer's mind into an entirely simulated biological state akin to watching a sunset. "Something really critical in my work is engaging someone's sense of wonder, and we have that when we're looking at a sunset or sunrise," he says. The interplay of his canvases and the specialized light will allow him to emulate what your body feels when watching a Tahitian sunset while standing in a windowless gallery high above the streets of Manhattan.

Working with a series of optical engineers, Stephen and Benjamin have developed a highly sensitive dimmer that can artificially imitate multitude wavelengths and the changes in sunlight's movement. Instead of walking into a room and flipping a simple on/off switch, owners of the dimmer will be able to download many different light sequences so they can have a romantic twilit dinner in a Moroccan dusk or wake up to the same wavelengths seen in the Scottish Isles. His team is currently measuring the light wavelengths around the world everywhere from Alberta, Canada, to Tasmania, Australia.

Aside from the romanticism of your body thinking it's waking up in the foothills of Nepal or the Italian Riviera, this artificial lamp could also be used to benefit those who don't have the privilege of experiencing a normal pattern of sunlight. "If you work until 3 a.m. and wake up at 10 a.m., there's no reason why you can't push your circadian rhythm back and program a dawn sequence for 9 a.m. and then turn your twilight mode on at 11 p.m.," Stephen explains. The same could be said for northern populations who never see the sun at all: By regulating their circadian rhythms and stimulating vitamin D production with these lights, it might help stave off SAD.

"It's absolutely the case that sunlight can be mimicked with the right technology; it's just that it hasn't been up until now. Our grandchildren are going to say, 'What do you mean the lights were either on or off? That's crazy!'" Benjamin says, laughing. "Once the technology is in place to control your light environment, it's going to be huge. It's such a fundamental quality of life issue that it's impossible to imagine a future where it's not part of the technological milieu."

As it turns out, our eyes don't really mind if light comes from a halogen lamp or the sun, as long as it provides them with the wavelengths they want, when they want. "If you're able to replicate a light spectrum, physiologically there will be no difference between the experience of that in nature or in a space with an artificial light source," Stephen says.

Stephen is by no means suggesting that we can have a happy lifestyle sitting in a room with a lamp that mimics light curves, but artificial lights could help us in times when nature's benefits aren't easily accessible. "I'm humbled by our innate relationship to nature, so I've always been suspicious of a technology claiming to replace the magnificence that nature provides," he says. "It took me some time to stop romanticizing, but I've begun to demystify light and look at it empirically:

It's a spectrum, it's a curve." The dimmer may be artificial, but it can bring us back to a baseline from which we can build a healthy emotional and physical state.

The irony of the artificial-versus-real-light dichotomy lies in the fact that we've become so hooked on the freedoms technology has afforded us that we might also need to use technology to set us right again. While it would be idealistic to suggest that we live by the light like we did for eons, rising and retiring with twilight and eating our granola at the same time every morning for the rest of eternity, what kind of existence would that be? Like most things in life, employing a little give and take will often lead us to optimal gratification (and will certainly be easier to uphold). Inventions such as Stephen's may allow us to reap sunlight's health benefits while still taking advantage of the joys that contemporary society allows us. We're never going to beat our bodies' yearning for routine and sunlight, but we can learn to work with them instead of against them. "We have trouble enough accepting that we turn into our parents, right?" Benjamin explains. "With circadian biology, we have four billion years of ancestry that we have to come to terms with."

The most important factor to consider when it comes to sensory well-being is figuring out what works best for you. Whether it's sleeping with a mask to help all your body's clocks align or programming an artificial dimmer to simulate a 6 a.m. dawn sequence in the depths of winter, even the act of being conscious about sunlight is a step in the right direction. As time goes on and the sun continues to rise and set every day until it flickers out, humans will continue to learn how to have a better relationship with it. There is still so much to discover, but at least we're beginning to see the light.

FOR MORE INFORMATION ON STEPHEN, BENJAMIN AND SUGGESTED READING MATERIALS, SEE PAGE 158.

GROUND (95.6)
1995
Color photograph on panel
16 ⅛ x 15 ⅛ inches, 41 x 38.5 centimeters

INTERVIEW
GAIL O'HARA

PHOTOGRAPH
LAURA BRAUN

THE LUMINARY

Danish-Icelandic artist Olafur Eliasson knows a thing or two about light:
He shone a giant sun in the center of London, made a moon with Ai Weiwei
and has helped provide portable solar lamps to thousands of people.

In 2003, Tate Modern commissioned Olafur to create the Weather Project, a giant sun in the massive Turbine Hall, which encouraged art watchers to lounge on the floor and bask in the blazing orange light. A creative powerhouse who engages his audience, he thinks about light in every possible way. We asked him a few questions about making art, projects he's been working on and what led to his luminous career.

What are some of your earliest memories of light and darkness? How did growing up in Iceland affect your perception of light? — When I was about five years old, I visited my grandparents in the city of Hafnarfjördur in Iceland. It was during the energy crisis of the '70s and I remember hearing a siren, and suddenly the whole city blacked out. It was an incredible feeling to see all the lights in a city go out at once, including the streetlights and gas stations. And strangely, in the summer, it was as if daylight had suddenly been turned on. When the lights went out, the twilight outside became much more prominent. This experience has influenced me and my artwork ever since. Light is something that pulls people together. It's a way of connecting people.

Why did you start making art? — I wanted to carry meaning into society. Art is a very good way of reconsidering reality not as something that's set and unchangeable, but as something that is relative. When I make something, I want it to be in the world. I want it to have an impact somehow.

Can you please tell us about your Little Sun project? — Little Sun is both the name of the solar-powered lamp I developed with solar engineer Frederik Ottesen and also the name of the company we set up to address the need for light in the off-grid areas of the world. And Little Sun isn't just about trying to get light to the 1.2 billion people around the world who lack adequate access to electricity—it's also an artwork. It's also about the feeling of having power: While working on Little Sun, Frederik and I discussed the idea that everyone in the world should be able to hold a bit of sunlight in their hand. We asked ourselves how we could give someone this feeling. It's also essential to Little Sun's approach that we focus on what we all have in common. We don't see the world as divided into "us" and "them." Little Sun is about what we all share as members of the global "we."

The Weather Project was something that allowed people to experience your work on a grand scale. How did it make you feel? — It was wonderful to see people lying on the floor in the Turbine Hall. That was more than ten years ago and Tate Modern had only just opened to the public. At the time, installations such as the Weather Project were very new. In art museums, you're normally meant to behave as a mute observer—you're not meant to participate in any way. But here people were not just interacting with the installation—they were coproducing it. The work arises through the viewers' encounters not only with the physical work and their surroundings, but also with each other in the space and with their own reflections in the mirror ceiling.

What reaction do you hope people have when they look at your art? — It's great when people from all sorts of backgrounds can feel welcomed by a single artwork. This is an incredible thought, and I resist telling people what to feel or think when looking at my work. Viewing art is one of those rare moments where we can all come together and share an experience—we can agree and we can disagree. Art is one of the few spaces in society where this is acceptable and even desired.

How do you light your own studio and home? — When we speak about light, we tend to think of it only as lighting a space to help us see. But light as energy is essential for life, and it works in many ways that we don't think about explicitly. On the roof of my Berlin studio, we store light in a small vegetable garden where we grow beans, sage, apple, mint, fennel, chard, zucchini, carrots, thyme, marjoram, oregano, rosemary, dill and chilies. The kitchen team transforms this energy into meals that the team eats together. Over the years the kitchen has become a central part of my studio, and you might say that the kitchen lights my studio and illuminates the thoughts of the team.

How have you seen light used in other people's work that has impressed you? — I've recently completed a series of experimental paintings devoted to the colors in the work of English painter J.M.W. Turner. I was struck at a young age by the works of Turner and his incredible ability to shape and frame light in his paintings. I find it interesting that he seemed to seek whatever truth there is in visual representation through the careful observation of external phenomena and the way we perceive light and color.

Can you talk about some of your recent projects based around light? — I'm showing new works at Tate Britain inspired by Turner's paintings. The exhibition grew out of experiments that deal with analyzing pigments and paint production to formulate a new color theory. The works isolate the sense of ephemera in Turner's work and his obsession with light and color. Each work is unique, but all are attempts at developing what I hope will evolve into a dynamic new color theory.

Turner Colour Experiments *will be on view through January 25, 2015, at Tate Britain, London.*

WORDS
JOANNA HAN

THE LIGHT BRIGADE

No one thinks about the way light affects us in spaces more than those who work with it. Meet three lighting designers who think in fresh ways and create products we covet.

ARIK
LEVY

NATHALIE
DEWEZ

MICHAEL
ANASTASSIADES

↓ "Beauty Mirror" (2010): A sleek round wall mirror available in gold- or nickel-plated stainless steel.

↓ "Tube Chandelier" (2006): A modern chandelier in black patinated or satin brass stainless steel.

↓ "Tip of the Tongue" (2013): A polished brass table lamp featuring a mouth-blown opaline sphere and a silk braided flex.

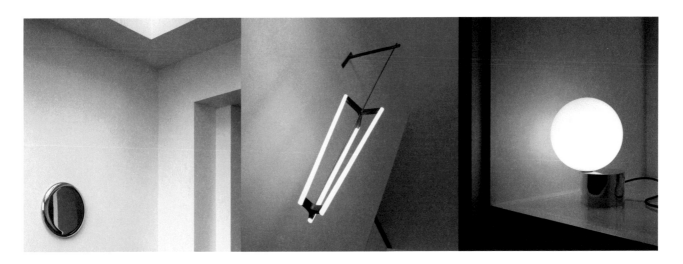

MICHAEL ANASTASSIADES

Originally from Cyprus, this designer has been creating utilitarian, conceptual work that encourages a dialogue between object and viewer in his London studio.

MICHAELANASTASSIADES.COM

What is it about working with light that interests you most? — You're addressing an object that must work in two scenarios: when the light is on and when the light is off. I was interested in the architectural aspect of this view—space, and the light that occupies that space. They're completely different, and I like that duality somehow.

Where do you find inspiration for your work? — I'm very interested in theater, psychoanalysis and human behavior, so I've always explored and drawn inspiration from these subjects. I was especially interested in the psychological relationship between the object and its user in my early work. For instance, my "Antisocial Light" only goes on when there's absolute silence. It will dim when you start talking around it, so you have to respect it in order to get what it can offer you. It creates a complex relationship that's not straightforward or easy.

What's the relationship between light and people? — We started looking at light as a practical way of being able to see. You have the daylight, and then at night you find other ways of illumination to continue your activities. It's a very primitive way of addressing the need for lighting. But I was once told something by a good architect friend of my father's that always stuck in my mind: He said, "There's a reason why there's the day and there's the night, and we should never try to replace or imitate one with the other." This made me realize it's about something a lot deeper than I originally thought, and that it's not really about solving a practical issue. There are a lot of elements that make light very special beyond its pure function of illumination. It's a very poetic, powerful medium.

↓ "Alwin" (2013): A balancing table lamp with a half-sphere base and a lightweight aluminum shade.

↓ "Olé!" (2013): A powder-coated aluminum and steel lamp named after its wide, sombrero-like disc.

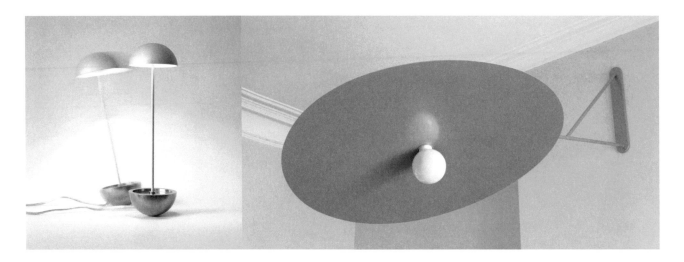

NATHALIE DEWEZ

Known for her elegant, efficiently designed works, this Brussels-based lighting designer creates high-end products and installations in art museums.

NATHALIEDEWEZ.COM

What first attracted you to lighting design? — The minute I pass through the door to a public space, I'll know if I'll be comfortable in there or not. When you enter a space, you'll behave very differently if you have a light focused on you than if it's indirectly focused on the ceiling. I find this relationship between light and space interesting.

Would you please describe your design process? — I really think that the more personal a work is, the more universal it will be. I try to position myself as the user, and I also think about context.

What considerations do you take when designing a lamp? — Lamps have something magical about them as they have two lives: During the day the object isn't used, and when lit up in the evening the lamp transforms itself and the space around it. It's really important to consider the formal aspect of the product as much as its functional aspect—lamps should be designed as a three-dimensional volume that's confronted by the space and by us, like a sculpture.

Who inspires you? — Alexander Calder, Ellsworth Kelly, Donald Judd, Dan Flavin, Daniel Buren, James Turrell, Yves Klein and Sol LeWitt.

Do you have any tips for creating warmth at home during winter? — Multiply the light sources: an indirect light to illuminate a white wall, a direct light for your armchair for reading, a soft pendant light above your table and another indirect light for your ceiling to enlarge your room. You'll never find one lamp that serves every purpose in different contexts. The balance of all these will create a pleasant atmosphere.

↓
↓
↓

"Globe" for Forestier (2014): A table lamp featuring a spherical form atop a hexagonal metal, cork or wood base.

"Moon" for Forestier (2014): A simple, partially opaque glass candleholder with a metal or wood base.

"Ness" for Vibia (2013): A minimal pendant lamp with dimmable LED lights. Made in graphite gray and off-white.

ARIK LEVY

This Israeli-born, Paris-based multidisciplinary artist and designer creates work that borders on fine art and industrial design in a variety of geometric shapes.

ARIKLEVY.FR

What is the importance of light to our lives? — No light means no architecture, no shadow, no perspective, no depth, no plants, no ambiance, no spirituality, no vision, no security and no communication. Light is fundamental in all aspects of our lives; creating a light isn't just about creating a light source in a shade.

What interests you most about lighting design? — I'm fascinated by the quality of the light and the associations an object can give to its user. I don't always know where I'm going with a design until I test it out in real life by closing doors during the day or staying in the studio late at night. This way I can see what the light will do to my mind and spirit, and see whether it will draw a smile. It's very important to consider what it is when the light is off.

How can we manipulate light to change a space? — It's more a feeling that I get that can't be translated into words, but it's clear that if you select the wrong light for a room, even if it's well designed, it can affect the space in the wrong way. The height, intensity, location, volume and quality of a light can help or destroy a space. Enjoy experimenting with lights in a room and you will see their effect.

Where do you find inspiration for your work? — I'm inspired by action, observation, social codes, nature, rawness, recreation, people and art. Design doesn't inspire me— I just create it.

How do you create warmth at home in the wintertime? — Be with people you like. The world is about people, and people are the real light we have.

ARTWORK & PHOTOGRAPHS
ANDERSEN M STUDIO

AURORA FOLKLORE

The northern lights have awed communities through the eras, and many fantastical theories have been imagined to explain the sky's shifting glow. We explore some of these light beliefs through the art of shadow puppetry.

FINNISH

This northern nation still calls the aurora borealis *revontulet*, which literally translates to "fox fire." Legend says that an arctic fox dashed across the tundra swiping snow up into the sky, while others claim his bushy tail caused sparks

NORSE

According to Norse mythology, female spirits called Valkyries chose who lived and
died in battle. They escorted the most heroic who fell to Valhalla, the "hall of the slain,"
which was overseen by Odin. The Vikings believed the lights were the reflection of the
Valkyries' armor and shields as they led the dead to their final resting place.

SWEDISH

In ancient Sweden, the term for the northern lights was *sillblixt*, which translates to "herring flash." They believed the aurora was caused by the reflections of light off the scales of large shoals of fish swimming in the sea. If a fisher spied the sillblixt, it was considered a prophetic sign they were about to stumble upon a particularly large haul.

DANISH

Danish legend speaks of the swans that held a competition to see who could
fly the farthest north. Some birds became caught in the ice and tried to escape by
flapping their wings. This flurry produced the waves of the aurora borealis.

INUIT

Perhaps the most playful explanation for the sky's colorful ripples comes from the indigenous populations of North America and Greenland: They both believed the lights came from the spirits of the dead in the afterlife playing soccer with a walrus skull.

WORDS
TRAVIS ELBOROUGH

SOLSTICE TRADITIONS

SHAB-E YALDA

IRAN — In pre-Islamic times, ancient Persians feared losing the sun to the forces of evil during the long black night following the shortest day of the year. To encourage the sun in its battle, they lit bonfires. Families and friends would then gather at each other's houses to hold all-night prayer vigils around a low square table called a *korsi* and, as the sun rose, they'd celebrate the triumph of light over darkness and the prospect of warmer weather. This nocturnal fiesta on December 21 was called the *Shab-e Yalda* and involved feasting on dried nuts, grapes, yogurt, watermelons, pumpkins and pomegranates. The ancient Persians believed that eating summer fruits such as watermelon would ward off sickness in the remaining cold months, and the pomegranate seeds were a reminder of the cycle of life (the Syriac word *yalda* means birth). Contemporary Iranians of all faiths keep Shab-e Yalda alive. It's a great excuse for a rowdy gathering where stories are exchanged, jokes told, songs sung and verses by the classical Persian poet Hafiz recited. Meanwhile, the menu has expanded to include lavish dishes of eggplant stew, saffron rice, chicken and spiced halva.

SOYAL

NORTH AMERICA — Across the globe, wheels are commonly used as symbols for the sun: The spokes represent its rays, and a spinning wheel mimics the sun's passage through the sky. Our yule, the title of the pagan solstice in Northern Europe and now loosely applied to the winter holiday season, quite possibly derives from the old Norse *hul*, meaning wheel. Similarly, the sun and the wheel are central to the *Soyal* festivities of the Hopi (the Peaceful Ones) of Arizona. This ceremony marks a key point in what they call "The Wheel of Life" when the sun "turns back" toward summer. The Hopi also welcome the return of the Kachinas, the cosmic spirit messengers who spend winter in the mountains communing with the dead (rather than skiing, as we might). In the days leading up to Soyal, prayer sticks called *paho* are woven together from *piñon* (pine) needles and feathers, and every man, woman, child, pet and property is purified using them. The rituals are concluded with exuberant public chanting, singing and dancing led by masked men dressed as Kachinas wearing bright body paint and decorated with feathers. The dance is a tribute to the gods of rain and fertility.

Mention sun worship today and we probably think of someone on a beach towel with a bottle of Hawaiian Tropic. But in the ancient world, the sun and moon were worshipped as gods. Solely dependent on their daily comings and goings, humans observed how these heavenly bodies waxed and waned as the seasons slipped from winter to summer. The longest and shortest days of the year (called the solstices, from the Latin for "sun stands still") therefore became pivotal dates in the earliest calendars. The midwinter solstice was universally regarded as especially magical. While we may no longer worship the sun as such, traces of this winter rite endure in festivities around the world.

DONGZHI

CHINA AND TAIWAN — Human beings are bipods and—as the Biblical story of Noah's ark also illustrates—we have something of a habit of pairing things off. Two was certainly company enough when the ancients in China divined that there were two essential forces at work in the world: yin and yang. The former was characterized by the moon: dark, watery, cold and passive. The latter was the sun: bright, expansive and muscular. Accordingly, the Chinese divided their year up between these opposing but complementary powers. Astrologers noted that yang rose after the winter solstice, and *Dongzhi*, the festival in its honor, was established around the time of the Han Dynasty (206 B.C.–220 A.D.). In centuries past it was a time of rest and reflection when special gifts, offerings and prayers were given to distant ancestors and recently departed relatives. Today in some regions of China, families gather to enjoy a hearty meal of dumplings, but the Dongzhi staple is normally *tāngyuán*—glutinous rice balls served in syrup or a sour broth. Their spherical form is intended to evoke the sun, the harmony of the seasons and the sense of wholeness from being reunited with the family.

LUCIADAGEN

SWEDEN — In the Roman Catholic tradition, St. Lucia is the patron saint of eye diseases. Lucia, a beautiful fourth-century maiden from Syracuse, Sicily, was supposedly blinded before being condemned to death for rejecting the advances of a heathen nobleman. Already treated to two saints days in her native Italy (May 1 and December 21), Lucia also has a crucial place in Sweden's calendar on December 13. *Luciadagen* (Lucia's Day), a jamboree of candles and light victuals, provides the Swedes with a well-needed chance to shake off some winter gloom. It begins with enchanting processions of young girls led by a homecoming queen–like leader acting as a modern-day incarnation of Lucia. The leader and her attendants carry burning white candles while wearing long white dresses with crimson sashes and lingon-leaf crowns in their flowing blonde hair. The girls sing a special St. Lucia song and distribute trays of hot coffee and *lussekatter* ("Lucia cats," which are saffron-and-cardamom-flavored buns) to their family, friends, neighbors, hospitals, the elderly and the needy. Variations abound but girls, lighted candles, coffee and cakes are the standard for the day's festivities.

INTI RAYMI

PERU — The axis of the earth, that imaginary line between the North and South Poles, is tilted from true north by some 23.5 degrees, meaning that the Southern Hemisphere experiences its shortest day in late June. Located firmly south of the equator, the Incas of Peru have an event called *Inti Raymi* to celebrate the Incan New Year and the solstice by honoring Inti, the sun god who resides in their imperial capital Cusco. Historically celebrated on June 24 and preceded by days of fasting and the scattering of flowers on the city's streets, Inti Raymi was once an extremely bloody affair, culminating in the sacrificial slaughter of llamas (and quite possibly the occasional human as well). Outlawed by the Spanish in the 16th century, Inti Raymi was officially revived in the 1940s. The highlight of the day is a grand procession that requires lugging two hefty golden thrones bearing the Sapa Inca, the divine ruling king, and his wife up in the hills high above Cusco. It now flourishes as a major annual tourist attraction in a form that retains all the glitz: Imagine vast entourages of robed high priests and jewelry-bedecked nobles, but without the gore. Even the llama sacrifice is artificially staged.

PHOTOGRAPHS
ROKAS DARULIS

STYLING
RACHEL CAULFIELD

Covering

our

Commute

*No matter the method of our daily comings and goings,
enduring peak-hour train schedules, frosty winds and claustrophobic
buses can be made all the more bearable with a good coat,
a decent book and a patient traveling companion.*

FOR CLOTHING CREDITS,
PLEASE TURN TO PAGE 158

THE THATCH HOUSE
136

THE EVERGREEN COTTAGE
140

THE COMMUNITY HALL
144

Home Tours:
Light

Light is one of the most important things to consider when choosing a place to live. This series takes us on a journey to three homes where light is key: We look into an architect's summerhouse in Korshage, Denmark, a festive house in a cobblestoned corner of Copenhagen and a quirky former community hall in Melbourne, Australia.

JACOB LONGBAEK & TRINE KORSHAGEN
1960 SUMMERHOUSE
KORSHAGE, DENMARK

WORDS
ANNA PERLING

PHOTOGRAPHS
WICHMANN + BENDTSEN

The Thatch House

"We come here to be someone else," Jacob Longbæk says about the Korshagehus, a summer home designed by his father-in-law (and famed Danish architect) Erik Korshagen. "You normally don't allow yourself to just meditate about who you are when you're in the middle of work or in town. This is the perfect place for that." Jacob and Trine took over the family home in 1998. Each summer they return to the town of Korshage, which is located on a peninsula an hour and a half north of Copenhagen, to enjoy the solitude of the forest and the calls of the seabirds from the nearby coast. Featuring a thatched roof, an unusual floor plan and a Japanese influence, the Korshagehus

has been deemed a protected historical home. Although they can't alter the exterior, the couple says the 1960 home is still in perfect condition and doesn't need renovating. "When the house was built, there were no doors between the rooms," Jacob says. "There's also a boardwalk all the way around the outside of the house. The idea was that this is a summerhouse, so you should be outdoors as much as possible." The dark interior, a result of the overhanging roof, encourages the couple to get out into the forest as often as possible. "You sit in the dark and watch the light," he says about being inside the house. "It's like going to the cinema—the landscape is lit." Existing in nature allows for

meditation, as does the home's unusually high doorsteps. "Being elevated gives you this ship-like feeling that you're floating in the middle of the forest," he says. "You're in a world by yourself—anchored, but only loosely. You could always float away." Jacob believes simplicity provides the best background for adding creative and personal touches to a space. "If you keep the furniture very simple, you always need a centerpiece, some oddity," he says. "The centerpiece is the focal point. It's something that gives the room personality. When people open the door, they have to be able to say, 'Ah, I'm home!' And if their home is decorated exactly like thousands of others, it's not really home."

Above: Børge Mogensen FDB chairs sit around a pine table in the warm dining room, designed by acclaimed Danish architect Erik Korshagen, who also designed the summerhouse. Right: The port window in the sauna room came from a boat.

MARIE WORSAAE
1900s SINGLE-STANDING HOUSE
COPENHAGEN, DENMARK

WORDS
BRIANNA KOVAN

PHOTOGRAPHS
PETER KRAGBALLE

The Evergreen Cottage

"The character of the house is so strong. I feel very humble that I'm allowed to live here and lucky to be a part of it and its history," says Marie Worsaae, co-owner of the Danish knitwear line AIAYU. Located in the Frederiksstaden district of Copenhagen, where most of the houses are historically protected, her home sits near both the city and the harbor. The neighborhood's architecture is asymmetrical and playful, reminiscent of the late-Baroque period. "It's in the city, yet it's airy and very calm," she says. "I love to be here on my own." Marie's home reflects her relaxed and minimalist style: The bare walls are calming and the open spaces are gentle and comforting, which provides solitude from the busy city streets and her social schedule. While she enjoys local markets and bakeries, her home is still her retreat away from the hustle and bustle. "I feel like I'm alone in the city with no noise other than the sound of birds and my neighbors playing a tune," she says. When Copenhagen's short winter days steal away the light, Marie truly appreciates the large windows and open lighting in her space. Each room was designed with light in mind: It's easy to rearrange the furniture to make the most of it during Denmark's winters. She decorates her house with a curator's eye and a focus on the past. Just as Marie situates herself within the building's history, she brings bits of her own life into the space: Her favorite furniture and decorations hold memories from loved ones, such as the Gustavian chairs from her late uncle. These chairs remind her of the moments that have shaped her life. Her advice for other homeowners to decorate would be this: "Be patient and don't try to put your home together too quickly," she says. "A home that feels patiently decorated gives a better feeling of the person who lives there and that person's journey through life."

Above: Marie received this Czech figure from her late uncle. While it's not traditionally a Christmas decoration, it has become one in her family. **Right:** Marie's father made her this nativity scene. "We're not that religious in our family, but we're very keen on stories and history," she says.

GEORGIE & AL CLEARY, PINO DEMAIO,
VIRGINIA MARTIN & BABY WREN
1922 FORMER COMMUNITY HALL
MELBOURNE, AUSTRALIA

WORDS
ANNA PERLING

PHOTOGRAPHS
JAMES GEER

The Community Hall

After siblings and business partners Georgie and Al Cleary moved into the old community hall that's now their home in Melbourne, Australia, they spent two years renovating the space with help from architect friends Jen Berean and Quino Holland. "We loved the fact that it was rundown as it gave us a chance to make the building our home," she says. Al even apprenticed as a builder's assistant during the construction, working on-site every day. But these two weren't strangers to the remodeling process. "When we were teenagers living on a rose farm, we bought an old house that was getting demolished and moved it on a truck to our property," she says. The brother and sister duo now runs the fashion brand Alpha60 and have added Al's partner Virginia Martin, Georgie's partner Pino Demaio and a 20-month-old child named Wren to their family. For this project, the redesign focused on light. They knocked down a wall to put in bifold doors that open up to the garden and moved a staircase that was blocking a light-filled window. When buying or redoing a home, Georgie and Al offer a wise adage: "Be flexible and enjoy the process." The quirky, larger-than-life pieces that characterize their home came later: a giant pair of polystyrene white Nike shoes, a stage piano hanging from the ceiling and a whale bone found by Pino's father. The decor's theatrical whimsy harks back to the house's prior incarnations. "When we bought the house, it had a stage in it," she says. "I've been told it was used for performances and dances." Built in 1922, the space also once housed a Chinese medicine practice: "A lady knocked on the door the other day and told me our home has good energy," she says. Located in the Westgarth area, the house is close not only to the city but to a charming old cinema and an organic grocery store. "We love it here," says Georgie. Although they love opening their house up to others, they treasure the times they get to spend there with family. "We feel at home when everyone is cooking and Wren is running and singing in the background," she says.

Above: The Coke bottles were found under the house when they restumped it. Right: The artworks in the corridor are by Alex Penfold and Rob McLeish. The brick wall, beams and door are all original. "There are a lot of bikes in our home. It's great to be able to hang some up!" Georgie says.

SOUTH EAST LONDON,
UNITED KINGDOM

WORDS
JAMES CARTWRIGHT

PHOTOGRAPHS
HELEN CATHCART

Neighborhood: Peckham

In the past decade this community in South East London has seen some pretty dramatic changes. Home to art colleges, small businesses and a vibrant local community, Peckham is one of the most transformed parts of the city. We enlisted someone who's been living there all along to tell us about the neighborhood's history and to point us in the direction of a good coffee.

In 1973, local artist Tom Phillips began an annual project documenting 20 different sites around Peckham, a district in South East London that once had an unsavory reputation. Using a pencil and compass, he drew a circle on the map that measured a half-mile radius from his home on Grove Park in the western part of town, marked 20 locations on the line and set off with his camera. Every year since then he has returned to those sites on the same day at the same time—on his own or with his son—to photograph them again, effectively building an evolutionary picture of the neighborhood he's called home for almost 50 years.

As far as native Londoners are concerned, Peckham has always had an unenviable status. It lacked the wealthy class of the city's west, the limitless opportunity of Central London, the leafy quiet of the north and the scrappy charm of the East End. It was also once a notoriously dangerous part of town to visit, with crime and gang-related violence occurring at a higher rate than in many other areas of London.

Tom's earliest images represent a town that's almost unrecognizable today. Where a disheveled hardware store stood in 1973 there is now a beautiful café selling delicious breads and excellent coffee. In the place of a grimy boozer there is an always-packed pub offering a vast range of craft beers. And on the site of a once-dilapidated newsagent now stands a world-renowned emporium of Persian culinary delights that supplies restaurants such as Ottolenghi and Moro.

Peckham is no stranger to this kind of change. The neighborhood was a lush pastoral hunting ground in the Middle Ages that became a bustling center of retail in Victorian times. More recently it's grown from being one of the most underprivileged suburbs of '80s London to a cultural destination to which the British media continually devotes column inches. As its fortunes have risen and fallen over the years, these changes are still evident in the architectural landscape: On some roads the atmosphere remains one of faded glory, filled with formerly gleaming art deco buildings that have worn with time. Their ground floors are packed with salons and nail bars with Pentecostal churches perching above them. But step away from the main drag and you'll find yourself on quiet, leafy streets lined with Georgian terraced houses that are surrounded by huge parks and community gardens.

The interplay between these contrasting worlds is part of what makes Peckham special. On Rye Lane, the high street, you can buy goat meat and yams from a Nigerian grocer before heading out for single-origin coffee at Lerryn's café. Lose

1   Choumert Grove offers an example of Peckham's architectural blend.
2   The café at the South London Gallery is a great spot to catch up on a bit of reading.
3   A trio chats over coffee at Anderson & Co. on Bellenden Road.

CHOUMERT GROVE
DON BOROUGH OF SOUTHWARK

1

2

3

yourself in the domestic *wunderkammer* (cabinet of curiosities) of Khan's Bargain Ltd. (which sells everything from Iranian dried figs to plastic animals), and then visit an exhibition at the nearby Sunday Painter. The culturally diverse population makes its mark on the area through its shops, restaurants, religious buildings and traditional attire.

An integral demographic that has played a part in Peckham's evolution has been its student community. Situated between Camberwell College of Arts, Goldsmith's College and a campus of King's College London, the academic population from all three institutions has thrived in recent years. In particular, the students from Camberwell have been customers (and later owners) of many

businesses like galleries, bars, design studios and print houses. Similarly, the former location of Camberwell College is now home to South London Gallery, the most respected contemporary gallery south of White Cube Bermondsey.

A student at Camberwell between 1960 and 1963 himself, Tom has lived on the border of Camberwell and Peckham since his college days. The neighborhood has been a constant source of inspiration, and in 2001 he was one of three artists—along with Antony Gormley and John Latham—commissioned to produce works of art as part of a £60 million project to regenerate Peckham. Tom designed two ceramic murals declaring "We Love Peckham" in abstract type and a set of street lamps.

The government's intention was to revive tourism and trade to a suburb that had become dangerous and dilapidated, plagued by crime and poverty.

Thirteen years later, the community's regeneration plans have paid off, and what realtors now refer to as Bellenden Village is a hive of chic eateries and specialty retailers. There's a wealth of new places to eat and buy food, as well as an array of bookshops, vintage stores and even a place to have your dog shampooed (if you're that way inclined). Some businesses—such as Review, a bookshop run by local novelist Evie Wyld—have been going for years, quietly garnering cult followings and encouraging early interest in the area. Many others have opened their doors

1

2

more recently and have brought with them an incredible range of culture— quality food in particular.

For daytime visitors there's Melange, an artisanal chocolate shop run by French chocolatier Isabelle Alaya. Her products are made on-site and include milk and dark chocolate bars, cakes, thick hot chocolate and an impressive selection of raw and vegan products. Across the road, Flock & Herd Butchery offers some of the best meat south of Old Kent Road. Proprietor Charlie Shaw apprenticed at London's Ginger Pig and has made his new shop a popular destination for fine cuts in the area. His emphasis is on ethical meat and making sure his animals have lived a privileged life, which has won him fans among locals and in the media.

If it's cheese and bread you're looking for, then the General Store should serve your needs well. Just a few doors down from Melange, it stocks an extensive range of cheeses from Neal's Yard Dairy, as well as sourdough loaves, fresh fruit and veg and traditional British baked goods. Anderson & Co. is another spot where you can sit back in the middle of bright, airy surroundings for some porridge, fresh pastries and a cracking cappuccino.

Outside of the culinary world, there's an eclectic range of vintage clothing to be found at Threads and a small but stylish collection of contemporary women's clothing at Bias. Another recent addition to Peckham's landscape is Rye Wax, a record and comics store specializing in rarities and secondhand

vinyl. It's arguably a clear sign that the population is changing, with the niche interests of the creative community now being catered to locally.

As the daytime trade dries up and the cafés close their doors, the parents and professionals that occupy the local shops from 9 to 5 are replaced by a younger, more mischievous crowd. There's still great food to be found, and the most respected venue to emerge recently has been the Begging Bowl, a Thai street food restaurant serving exquisite soups, salads, endless steamed rice and imaginative updates on traditional dishes. Its location in Bellenden Village has been cursed until now: A French brasserie, a Caribbean bakery and a pizzeria run by Canadians all failed to find a captive audience, but the Begging Bowl seems

3

to have bucked that trend. Locals may grumble about the high prices but it's unlikely you'll find anything else like it around here.

Peckham has some pedigree when it comes to good food. One of its most celebrated culinary destinations is run by the youngest in a line of British food legends. Frank Boxer is the proprietor of the Campari bar and restaurant called Frank's, which is situated on the rooftop of a former parking garage and receives high praise year after year. Patrons enjoy incredible views across London's skyline from St. Paul's Cathedral and the Shard in the center of town to the high-rise financial island of Canary Wharf in the east. The lines can spill out regularly onto Rye Lane below, but it's worth the sometimes hour-long wait to see the

skyline from up above. Frank is a talented chef in his own right, but he comes from good stock: His grandmother Arabella Boxer wrote the iconic *First Slice Your Cookbook* in the mid-'60s, her son Charlie, Frank's father, runs a deli in nearby Vauxhall that offers the finest Italian ingredients in town, and Frank's brother, Jackson, owns the Brunswick House Café, which specializes in traditional English fare with a contemporary twist.

Frank's is also the watering hole for Bold Tendencies, an annual visual and performing arts festival that fills the top four floors of the garage with installations every summer, commissioning local and international artists to produce site-specific works of art. The food Frank serves has played a large part in Bold Tendencies' sculptural success, with his

plates of ox hearts, smoked paprika corn on the cob and huge slabs of cheese keeping the tourists sated. What started as a ramshackle enterprise in 2007 has grown into a slick operation and an essential destination for Londoners both north and south. Of course the sculptures on display during the summer are a massive draw, but it's hard to deny the appeal of swilling negronis in the evening sun, no matter what.

Like most watering holes in Peckham, Frank's closes at 11 p.m., so it's best to leave early and get seats at the Montpelier on Choumert Road, one of the few places nearby with a license that stays open past midnight. The largely residential neighborhood prohibits all-night drinking and after-hours revelry, so you'd be wise to find a local who can

5

1

2

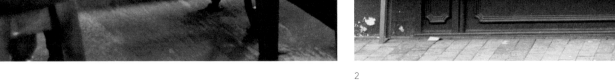

4

5

ERAL STORE 174

PROVISIONS

1 The Montpelier on Choumert Road offers
  top-notch spirits and bar snacks.
2 Like much of Peckham, the simple design of
  the General Store is classic and practical.
3 Butchers from Flock & Herd take pride in
  their fine products.
4 The Camberwell College of Arts offers a
  quiet place to relax.
5 Passersby admire the General Store's
  selection of produce through the window.

3

direct you to a house party afterward, if that's your intent. Otherwise, there is dancing to be had all night at the Bussey Building, a club in a former munitions factory that also functions as both an art café and rooftop cinema.

Peckham's increasing popularity has been a mixed blessing for the area. On one hand it brings jobs and entertainment to its residents, but on the other it drives property prices up, forcing the existing communities further out into the suburbs. Of course, this is a problem all over both the city of London and the rest of the world.

The Peckham Refreshment Rooms is a new restaurant and wine bar that understands the pressure of development well. They've been open for just over a year, but their Blenheim Grove site is at the heart of council plans for a luxury housing development. After they invested £50,000 into opening their business, the owners were told that their building would be demolished.

Ironically, it's these very businesses that have made Peckham attractive to developers again in the first place, but their success threatens to uproot them in favor of plush flats. The supportive response from the community has been fierce and unreserved, but a petition designed to halt the demolition has only delayed the council's plans for another year. As a result, the threat of closure looms large for some of the area's most exciting new enterprises, including a gallery, screen printers and a brand-new brewery—all of which are located on a single street.

However, if the area's history is anything to go by, it's likely that these vibrant hubs in Peckham's cultural community will be saved by the locals. All the way back in 1868, St. Giles' Church in Camberwell bought an area of land known as Peckham Rye to save it from becoming a housing development. To this day it remains a vast public park in the south end of town and is now home to a wonderfully picturesque Japanese garden and a local flock of bright green parakeets. If that location hadn't been saved more than a century ago, then the area would have become one giant urban sprawl. Hopefully this will set a precedent for the continued success of the neighborhood, and we'll see sites on Tom's photographic map of Peckham flourish in years to come.

Kinfolk Gatherings

In 2014, the Kinfolk community hosted more than 60 events in locations from Madrid to Mexico City. We cannot say thank you enough to our hosts, partners and attendees for making these special dinners possible around the world.

PHOTOGRAPHS
(Left) Tokyo: Hideaki Hamada
(Right) Sydney: Luisa Brimble

For *Kinfolk*'s first gathering of the year, we celebrated our summer edition, the Saltwater Issue, by looking to the sea as our muse. Whether only yards from the shore or in a landlocked nation, we welcomed the season with a meal inspired by *L'esprit de la Mer* (the Spirit of the Sea) and the delectable and beautiful bounty the oceans provide. For our second gathering, we took inspiration from our autumn edition, the Imperfect Issue, for a series of wabi-sabi-inspired events that embraced life's unique qualities through innovative dishes and a respect for nature's whims.

Kinfolk's dinner series will continue in 2015 with increased frequency in big cities and small towns alike. For news on upcoming locations, tickets and other gathering details, please check our online events page. We hope you can join us at a *Kinfolk* event in your community soon!

www.kinfolk.com/events

Event-related inquiries are warmly welcomed at:
community@kinfolk.com

ISSUE FOURTEEN CREDITS

SPECIAL THANKS
*Thanks to Sarah Jacoby for the Starters
and Winter illustrations*

ON THE COVER
Photograph Neil Bedford
Model Emily Meuleman at
Elite Models London
Styling Rose Forde
Assistant Styling Indigo Goss
Production We Are Up Production
Casting Simon Lewis at Cast & Elect
Retouching Oliver Carver and
Tomika Davis
Hair Aimee Hershan at
Stella Creative Artists
Makeup Lyz Marsden at Caren
Clothing Coat by Stutterheim; turtleneck
by Goal & Related/Goal Library; trousers
by Aquascutum; bag by Parka London;
umbrella by London Undercover

BEFORE THE DAY STARTS
Photograph Tao Wu

WINTER'S KITCHEN
COLORING THE GRAY
A CUP OF GOODWILL
UNEXPECTED PAIRINGS
LEADERS OF THE PACK
Illustrations Katrin Coetzer

TINSEL TUSSLE
Photograph Parker Fitzgerald
Model Joanna Han
Clothing Shirt by Henrik Vibskov;
jeans by Acne Studios, both courtesy
of Table of Contents
*Special thanks to Plumper Pumpkin Patch
and Tree Farm*

SHAPE SHIFTERS
Artwork Merijn Hos
Photographs Anja Verdugo

MY BEDSIDE TABLE
Photograph Parker Fitzgerald

LUNCH BOX: TURKEY SANDWICH
Photograph Alice Gao
Food Styling Diana Yen
Prop Styling Kate S. Jordan
Lunch boxes by Potager

ALL WOUND UP
Photograph Rahel Weiss
Styling Rose Forde
Assistant Styling Indigo Goss
Models Kate Howat and Kit Reeve
at Elite Models London
Hair Patrick Forini
Makeup Kamila Forini
Clothing (Left) Dress by Margaret
Howell; camel scarf by COS; lilac scarf by
Folk; mustard scarf by Toast. (Right) Dress
by MHL by Margaret Howell; navy and
gray scarf by GANT Rugger; pink scarf by
Folk; burgundy scarf by Margaret Howell

THE HUNGER GAMES
Assistant Food Styling Poppy Campbell

SOLE AND BRUSSELS SPROUTS
Photograph Anders Schønnemann
Food Styling Mikkel Karstad
Prop Styling Sidsel Rudolph

DUEL INTENTIONS
Assistant Styling Indigo Goss and
Marina Pamies
Special thanks to Darling Creative

Clothing
Page 58: Cape by APC; top by Uniqlo;
fencing trousers by Costume Studio;
mask from the National Theatre

Page 60: Top by COS; fencing trousers,
model's own

Page 61: (Left) Sweater by Scotch;
top by COS; fencing trousers by Costume
Studio; socks by American Apparel;
sneakers by Opening Ceremony for Adidas.
(Right) Jacket by Albam